STRATEGIC LEARNING
A Holistic Approach to Studying

STRATEGIC LEARNING
A Holistic Approach to Studying

Robert K Kamei, M.D.
National University of Singapore, &
Duke University, USA

Contributing author:
Magdeline Ng
National University of Singapore

NEW JERSEY • LONDON • SINGAPORE • BEIJING • SHANGHAI • HONG KONG • TAIPEI • CHENNAI • TOKYO

Published by

World Scientific Publishing Co. Pte. Ltd.
5 Toh Tuck Link, Singapore 596224
USA office: 27 Warren Street, Suite 401-402, Hackensack, NJ 07601
UK office: 57 Shelton Street, Covent Garden, London WC2H 9HE

Library of Congress Cataloging-in-Publication Data
Names: Kamei, Robert K., author.
Title: Strategic learning : a holistic approach to studying / Robert K Kamei.
Description: First. | New Jersey : World Scientific, [2021] |
    Includes bibliographical references and index.
Identifiers: LCCN 2020053611 | ISBN 9789811226632 (hardcover) |
    ISBN 9789811227776 (paperback) | ISBN 9789811226649 (ebook for institutions) |
    ISBN 9789811226656 (ebook for individuals)
Subjects: LCSH: Study skills. | Metacognition. | Strategic planning.
Classification: LCC LB1049 .K334 2021 | DDC 371.30281--dc23
LC record available at https://lccn.loc.gov/2020053611

British Library Cataloguing-in-Publication Data
A catalogue record for this book is available from the British Library.

Copyright © 2021 by World Scientific Publishing Co. Pte. Ltd.

All rights reserved. This book, or parts thereof, may not be reproduced in any form or by any means, electronic or mechanical, including photocopying, recording or any information storage and retrieval system now known or to be invented, without written permission from the publisher.

For photocopying of material in this volume, please pay a copying fee through the Copyright Clearance Center, Inc., 222 Rosewood Drive, Danvers, MA 01923, USA. In this case permission to photocopy is not required from the publisher.

For any available supplementary material, please visit
https://www.worldscientific.com/worldscibooks/10.1142/12001#t=suppl

Typeset by Stallion Press
Email: enquiries@stallionpress.com

"Dr. Robert Kamei brings a rich background to this highly valuable survey of learning. After pioneering work in reforming medical education, he developed for undergraduates a fantastic course on how to learn, and he has captured the deep insights of that experience in this wonderful volume. Easy to read and follow even complex ideas, this book will delight and inform students and teachers alike. Highly recommended."

Ken Bain
Historian and author of 'What the Best College Teachers Do' (Harvard University Press) and 'Super Courses: The Future of Teaching and Learning' (Princeton University)

"Learning scientists have done a good job of getting their findings to instructors to help them improve their teaching. But so much of learning is under the student's — and only the student's — control. Strategic Learning fills a critical need to educate students on what the field knows about how to learn productively. We should be getting it into the hands of every university student."

Lori Breslow
Senior Lecturer, MIT Sloan School of Management
Founding Director, MIT Teaching & Learning Laboratory

"*Strategic Learning* was an unexpected find. At first I was planning on reading some chapters that had been called to my attention and then wow – by the end of the evening I had read the book cover to cover. It is both strategic and holistic on how to learn most effectively by tuning into deep properties of your own mind. For example, once you have learned something how often do you review it and what is the ideal spacing you might want between reviews to really accelerate total mastery? Understanding some of these metacognitive findings helps us while in college, graduate school, or for lifelong learning at any age in our world of constant change. This book is a real find. Thank you Dr Kamei for taking the time to write it and to make it all seem so ease to put into practice."

John Seely Brown
Author, with Doug Thomas, 'The New Culture of Learning'
Co-founder of the Institute for Research on Learning (IRL)
Former Chief Scientist, Xerox Corporation
Director of Xerox Palo Alto Research Center (PARC)

"This is a just-in-time book for both teachers and students. Bob's comprehensive, strategic approach to learning has really made a difference in his students' learning experiences. Based on the evidence-based framework and easy-to-understand procedure, anyone who aspires to create optimal learning for themselves or for their children or students would be able to benefit from Bob's methodology — a holistic learning framework which can help overcome the learning myths that many believe in and build their new learning scenarios."

Yao-Ting Sung
Executive Vice President and Chair Professor
National Taiwan Normal University
Director, The National Assessment Center for Education in Taiwan

"Dr. Bob was our pediatrician. If we could trust him with our kids, you can trust him with how to learn better. I discovered many surprising truths about learning in this book, so follow the scientific research and become a better learner."

Guy Kawasaki
Bestselling book author, chief evangelist of Canva and creator of the 'Remarkable People' podcast

"Since the very start of VinUniversity, we have appreciated Prof Kamei's thoughtful advice on setting up our educational programs and active learning. With this book, he has turned his attention to advising students how best to learn. Now, they too can benefit from his educational insights and experiences. I suggest that all students, and faculty, consider reading his book to get the very most out of their university education."

Le Mai Lan
President of VinUniversity, Hanoi, Vietnam
Vice Chairwoman of Vingroup

"*Strategic Learning* is an outstanding book that has combined Bob's distilled expertise over decades of teaching with insights consolidated from the science of learning globally in a very readable and clear guide to optimising one's personal learning. Every student (and every educator) should read this!"

Jeremy Lim
Associate Professor, Director of the Leadership Institute
for Global Health Transformation Saw Swee Hock School
of Public Health, National University of Singapore
CEO of AMiLi (GI microbiome company)

"Universities are good at telling students what to learn, but much less so at how to actually do that. Kamei's *Strategic Learning* fills that gap. It begins with debunking popular myths about learning, then builds a deep understanding of the metacognitive and self-regulatory processes underlying learning, and concludes with tangible advice on how to put this into practice. And it's fun to read!"

Andreas Schleicher
Director for Education and Skills, and Special Advisor on
Education Policy to the Secretary-General at the Organisation for Economic
Co-operation and Development (OECD)
Oversees the Programme for International Student Assessment (PISA)

"Professor Robert K. Kamei teaches a popular course at NUS, which focuses on the science and techniques of learning better. He has compiled this exciting knowledge into a new book, *Strategic Learning*, for wider public understanding. Learning skills are increasingly important, not just to students, but also working adults, and all who are seeking to develop their potential to the fullest. In this era, we are all encouraged, and expected, to be learning constantly, and thereafter apply new knowledge in ever-changing circumstances. Professor Kamei's book shows that with practice and patience, we can all develop strong learning skills which can enhance our creativity, adaptability and resilience."

Professor TAN Eng Chye
President
National University of Singapore

"There is no single teaching and learning technique that can be applied effectively to every student. Learners should learn how to learn successfully, and teachers should know how to create proper learning environment. This book provides learners and teachers to understand and to be able to apply "STRATEGIC LEARNING" to achieve the real benefit of education."

Prasit Watanapa
Dean, Faculty of Medicine
Siriraj Hospital, Mahidol University, Thailand

Acknowledgments

I would like first to thank my colleague and contributing author: Magdeline Ng and other faculty members: Joshua Gooley, Mara McAdams and Jennifer Davis, for their contributions to my course at the National University of Singapore (NUS). Over the past several years, I have also been especially fortunate to work with many outstanding student teaching assistants. Their hard work and frank feedback have made our course and this book better.

As you will learn from this book, "to teach is to learn twice". It would not have been possible for me to write this book without the experiences I've had teaching students in Singapore and the United States. I benefited whenever I saw confused or disbelieving expressions on my students' faces; I knew I needed to figure out a better explanation. They had considerable influence on how I present the information in this book.

Special thanks to Tan Eng Chye and Ranga Krishnan, who first suggested that I try to pull together what I knew about the learning sciences into a course at NUS to help students become better prepared to learn. It was my experiences as the founding Vice Dean, Education at Duke-NUS Medical School that allowed me to implement my educational ideas and in turn, provided me valuable insights into student learning. My thanks to Sandy Williams (Duke-NUS Medical School's first dean), who had the faith to hire me and who allowed me to use science rather than tradition to set up our new school.

Acknowledgments

I want to mention several important academic mentors: William Schwartz (who has been a constant source of feedback and encouragement throughout my career), Larry Shapiro (who suggested at the start of my career that I learn more about the science of learning), and Abe Rudolph (who told me not to be afraid to expect the very best from my students). I have been fortunate to have great mentors, and my advice is that all learners should find and cultivate similar relationships.

Several people volunteered to read versions of this book and offered helpful comments and new perspectives. My special thanks to Thomas Kamei, Jeremy Lim, Xavier Chan, Doyle Graham, Bill Schwartz, Kat Maung, Rocky and Walker Chuppe.

There are many others to thank, but it could make this acknowledgment section longer than the rest of the book! However, I have saved my most precious for last. I am especially grateful for my parents (Tami and Hiroshi), Michelle, Thomas, Kenzi, and other loved ones who have supported me in countless ways throughout my life. The lessons I learned from them have been my true inspiration behind helping others become strategic learners.

Contents

Acknowledgments ix

Introduction 1
   Memory and learning 2
   The counterintuitive nature of learning: Easy is not always better 3
   The learning myths that we believe 3
   Why listen to me about learning? 6
   Everyone can benefit from learning better 8
   References 9

Chapter 1   The Holistic Learning Framework 11
   Metacognition (thinking about thinking) 12
   Learning to learn better is an individual journey 13
   A holistic approach 14
   Knowing the best way to learn is not enough 17
   Social determinants of learning 18
   References 19

Chapter 2   Setting Goals 21
   Setting more thoughtful goals 22
   How to make SMART goals 25
   SMART goals are not enough: Aspirational Goals 27

Contents

Goldilocks and getting things "just right"	30
References	35

Chapter 3 The Metacognitive Cycle — Recognition vs Recall   37

Why memorize anything?	38
Recognition versus Recall	40
The forgetting curve: 3 major features of how we remember and forget	45
References	47

Chapter 4 The Metacognitive Cycle — Encoding Memory   49

Encoding memory	50
Strategies to improve encoding	58
Attention	59
References	61

Chapter 5 The Metacognitive Cycle — Flattening Out the Forgetting Curve   63

Forgetting is not all bad!	64
Making additional connections	66
Depth of processing	67
Interleaving	69
Shallow versus deeper levels of processing	73
References	76

Chapter 6 The Metacognitive Cycle — Resetting the Forgetting Curve   77

Cramming works! (Sort of)	78
Not everything is equally important to re-learn	80
Implementing spaced learning	82
Retrieval practice	84
References	87

Contents

Chapter 7	**The Foundation — Self-Regulation**	**89**
	Self-regulation and self-discipline	90
	External versus internal motivation	92
	Procrastination	99
	References	104
Chapter 8	**The Foundation — Health and Wellbeing**	**107**
	Distractions from learning	110
	Is it multitasking or rapid task switching?	112
	Giving yourself a break	113
	The effect of exercise on learning	114
	The most significant impact on learning for most students: Sleep	115
	Other health issues	119
	References	120
Chapter 9	**Developing, Implementing and Evaluating a Learning Plan**	**123**
	Brainstorm for obstacles to your plan	125
	Learning with others	125
	Implementing your metacognitive learning cycle	128
	Evaluating your metacognitive cycle	129
	Failure is a great teacher	133
	Creating your personal learning plan	134
	Reference	136
Chapter 10	**Modernizing Education to Learn Better**	**137**
	How should education change?	139
	New approaches to teaching (such as a flipped classroom) and the learning sciences	142
	What can learners do if their teachers aren't willing or able to change their classrooms?	146
	Learning in the virtual classroom	147

Lessons from my father	149
Reference	152
Conclusion Final Thoughts on the Power of Thoughts	**153**
Growth mindset and stereotype threat	156
Your strategic learning approach	158
References	159
Appendices	161
Appendix A	161
Appendix B	162
Appendix C	164
Appendix D	166
Appendix E	176
Bibliography	177
Some Additional Information and Resources	183
Index	185

Introduction

Myth: Just like I naturally learned to walk and talk on my own, I naturally know how to learn.

Reality: The science of learning has revealed many findings that are counterintuitive. You need to overcome these learning myths to improve your study skills.

With the possible exception of Nobel Prize winners, as we go through school, it takes more and more work to get the same grades each year. The course work gets harder, and it feels increasingly impossible to keep up with the other bright students in class. Some people face this when they enter college, others earlier in their education or later in graduate school. Others struggle the most trying to keep up to date in their careers with the latest facts and technologies. For me, it happened several times: when I studied Japanese in college and when I first attended medical school. When did it happen for you?

Along with several faculty colleagues, I've been teaching one of the most popular undergraduate courses at the National University of Singapore (NUS): Learning to Learn Better. Our course is an elective, not a required course. Nevertheless, it was taken by over 1500 students last year. The undergraduates attending NUS are among the academic best in the world, so why would so many students be interested in learning how to learn?

Introduction

I find that most of my students are like how I was when I was younger: working hard, but not necessarily smart. Many of these students know that they could be learning better but don't know how.

Over the course of my career, I've worked with bright students from all over the world. These students, no matter what education system they were from, were also looking to learn better. Some brilliant students somehow figure out by themselves how to study optimally, but most require advice. And once students have a strategic approach to learning, one that helps them cope with any learning challenge they face, they do much better at achieving their academic goals.

Memory and learning

Students are often confused, thinking that learning and memory are the same. In fact, learning is different from memory, despite them being closely related.

Learning is an acquired skill or knowledge that takes time and work to achieve. Memory is an expression of learning but occurs almost instantaneously and lasts for variable amounts of time. Without memory, you cannot learn. And as you'll find out as you read this book, once you learn something, memory associated with that learning is improved.

Unfortunately, our education system doesn't emphasize the difference enough. Most teachers write examinations that test our memory. It is much harder to test for learning. But learning, not memory, is what it takes to succeed outside of school. That is one reason why many students considered smart in school don't live up to their academic potential. They might be good memorizers, but not necessarily good learners. What we learn is a critical aspect of our success. And what we can remember is a critical aspect of what we learn. We need both.

What makes both optimal memory and learning so tricky for people to figure out for themselves is that much about memory and learning is actually counterintuitive. It turns out that the scientific literature on this subject is pretty consistent and clear: Learners have a blind spot on what is optimal learning. We don't naturally understand how to learn best.

The counterintuitive nature of learning: Easy is not always better

Scientists have looked at the effect on learning when students read words printed using different fonts. Their surprising results provide an example of the counterintuitive nature of learning.

Imagine for a moment that someone offers you a choice to study one of two books. Although both books have the same words, one book has been published in a typeset that is much more difficult to read, and with faded lettering. In the other book, the words are bright, clear and easy to read. Which book would you prefer to read? If you are like me, it would be an easy decision to buy the book that is easier to read.

And you would probably bitterly complain if you had to read the book with the difficult-to-read typeset. But, as it turns out, when studied by researchers, the extra work it takes to understand a more challenging-to-read text makes you concentrate more. You have to process the words more deeply to be able to read them. You might even have to decipher an unintelligible word or two in the sentence. When they tested students on how well they learned material presented in a more difficult fashion, they typically did better! The psychological term for this finding is "cognitive dysfluency" (Alter, 2013; Diemand-Yauman, Oppenheimer, & Vaughan, 2011).

While I'm not ready to recommend that all textbooks should be hard to read, it does make two important points. That extra bit of work that it takes to read the material can make you remember the information better, not worse. And we have a difficult time recognizing when we are learning well.

The learning myths that we believe

As a result of our experiences, we have beliefs about learning that we tend to hold tightly, even though they aren't entirely true. Like all good myths, there is just enough truth in each one of them to convince us they are correct, even when they are wrong overall. For example, you might believe that you learn better from something easier to read. This is true to the extent that if a text is too hard to read, then many learners give up and learn nothing at all! For a dysfluent text to increase understanding, it has to be just hard enough to be challenging but not so hard as to be completely off-putting. Dysfluency is one example of how optimal learning can be counterintuitive.

These false beliefs or myths are applied widely in situations even when they are not valid and falling for them is an important reason why students don't learn optimally. I will emphasize these misconceptions by starting each chapter with a commonly held myth about learning.

I've learned from my professional experience helping thousands of students, and from my personal struggle to learn better, that students having trouble in school have a difficult time adapting and changing how they study. Because optimal learning is often counterintuitive, they have a hard time believing the scientifically proven methods to learn better. It is easy for them to get stuck with their old ways of studying, unable to make any adjustments in the way they learn. They need a strategic approach to improve their learning.

Some of these learning myths are very powerful and deeply ingrained. My experiences with students have taught me that convincing them to believe what we tell them about learning myths is not enough. Getting them to change their learning strategies is also like getting people to lose weight or stop smoking. Everyone understands the health benefits of losing weight, and there is plenty of advice on different diet regimes to try. But that knowledge doesn't mean you find it simple to change what you are doing and lose weight.

These students strongly believe they "know" what is best for them. When informed of the scientific literature, they often still insist that the published studies are wrong or somehow don't apply to them.[1] While some students are willing to admit that these techniques may be correct for most students, they still insist that they belong to the minority of those that aren't helped by them. If you are like most people, you too have some level of skepticism when it comes to the idea that reading a book printed in a font that is more

---

[1] I have chosen not to heavily reference this book with every relevant research paper possible. Instead I tried to achieve a balance of only including some of the most important or interesting reports that readers of this book might want to look up and read more about. Hopefully, this will serve as a good starting point for those interested in knowing more about this subject.

Introduction

difficult to read can result in higher, not lower comprehension. It just doesn't make sense to our brains.

For those of you who are like our students — skeptical and having a hard time believing what we are saying — I have re-created on our strategic learning website (www.strategiclearn.org) a few of the activities we developed for our classroom students. We use these experiences to demonstrate to students how these learning strategies specifically apply to them and can help them retain more knowledge for longer periods. You will find links to our strategic learning webpage activities in the relevant chapters. These supplementary online experiences will hopefully convince you that there are ways to improve your learning, even if you would not have previously believed it. Our strategic learning website blog is also a place to learn more about aspects of learning not covered in this book. And our online forum is a great place to post questions and comments for our learning community. We have also placed on our website some of the videos we made for our students to explain some of the learning concepts described in this book.

In our NUS course, we don't just tell our students which study strategies to use; we also teach them the science of learning that established these approaches as useful. As I worked to help my students learn, I realized even proving how strategies applied to them was not enough! I had to do more than impart my knowledge of the science of learning and demonstrate that it applies to them. My students also needed help to pull together these techniques to create a personal learning plan that works for them.

Keeping Track Of Your Learning Ideas Activity
(Approximate Duration: While Reading This Book)

Aim: Keeping track of your learning ideas

Instructions: Appendix A has a copy of the Holistic Learning Framework diagram that you will see throughout the book. Use the figure in Appendix A as a place to keep your notes on the ideas presented in this book that you would like to incorporate into your personal strategic learning plan. There are so many ideas presented in this book, you will lose track of them unless you can save your notes in one place! Hint: write the page number next to any idea to make it easy to refer back to.

Introduction

In addition to participating in our website learning activities, I encourage you to create a learning plan as outlined in this book. I have described this more completely in Chapter 10 and Appendix D. Your learning plan should incorporate the ideas that you believe will work best for you. The format of this plan is not as important as the planning itself. Many students also create a study calendar that translates their learning plan into specific dates and times; including when and where to study, as well as what learning activities they will utilize during that time. However, just writing a few ideas down on paper is a great start and a big step toward improving your learning.

Why listen to me about learning?

My academic career has been quite unusual. As well as having a successful medical practice, I have taught the practice of medicine to students for many years. I have also managed major teaching programs at the undergraduate and graduate university level.

As a result of my background in both medicine and education, I have also learned what science says about how to train my students best. I have been especially interested in the overlap of these two fields: the impact that health and well-being has on learning. For example, probably the most significant impediment to learning when it comes to our NUS undergraduates is not their poor study habits but rather, their poor sleep habits. It is hard to study when you are so tired! To help students learn better, they need more than just a few study tips. Instead they need a comprehensive, more holistic approach than most books on learning offer.

However, you may be surprised to hear what I consider my most significant credential for teaching a course on learning and writing this book. No, it is not that I attended top schools throughout my life, nor that I dedicated my career to helping others learn. Nor is it that I consider myself a naturally gifted, great learner, ready to pass along tips of how I achieved my academic success. Instead, I believe my most important credential is that I have always found myself a reasonably good but not a brilliant student.

Introduction

So, why on earth would you consider reading a book on learning from someone like that? Shouldn't you be learning instead from someone who naturally achieved the highest marks on all of their tests throughout their entire life?

In college, I dutifully went to ALL of my classes held for the courses I was taking at the time. While I knew that I didn't learn much from the lectures in class, I was afraid (even though my mind wandered during most of the lectures or I fell asleep!) that I was going to miss something important if I didn't attend.

Furthermore, I couldn't understand how my classmates, who were hardly going to any classes at all, were getting as good or better grades than me. What was their secret? Were they just much smarter than me? Going to class made me feel like I was doing my best, but I now realize that I wasn't doing my best. I didn't know how to make the best use of the educational methods my teachers used. I wasn't studying efficiently. I only kept up with the rest of my class because of "brute force." In other words, I simply willed myself to work harder than anyone else.

After I graduated with a bachelor's degree from Stanford University, I attended medical school at the University of California, San Francisco. Learning in medical school is often described as "drinking from a fire hose." Although I studied even harder than I did before, there was so much more to learn in medical school. I couldn't keep up, let alone study harder than everyone else. My previously successful study systems got overwhelmed and broke down; I couldn't get the same grades that I had achieved up to that time. Looking back at my experience, I now realize that I needed not to work harder, but to work smarter and more strategically. I just didn't know how to do it.

Learning how to learn was not part of my traditional, general education. As I developed as a professional educator, I found many previously successful, highly motivated students like myself suddenly in a situation where the amount of material was overwhelming, or the content to learn became more complicated. They would ask: "It worked before, so why not now?" Because

Introduction

Figure 1. Have you ever found yourself completely overwhelmed with everything you are expected to learn? You are not alone.

of this, some crashed academically, and, unfortunately for too many, this often resulted in a personal crisis as well. They weren't willing to take a chance on learning in new ways they were not used to and especially ways that they didn't fully believe in.

As I taught my students, I recognized how easy it was to be fooled by common misconceptions about how to learn best. My contributing author, Magdeline Ng, has included some stories from our students of how they were helped by learning more about learning. There is no need to feel alone in your learning journey; many others have also struggled but learned how to learn better and achieved greater academic success.

Everyone can benefit from learning better

Although I'm sure university students will find this book pertinent to them, there is considerable research that indicates that learners at all ages can benefit in multiple ways from learning new things and learning to learn better (Ball *et al.*, 2002). And for those teachers reading this book, your perceptions are no different from those of your students! Despite their long experiences in education, teachers still hold on to many of the same learning myths as the rest of us. As a result, many teachers possess the same stiff resistance to changing how they learn for themselves and how they teach their students. No wonder it is so challenging to improve educational practice in our school systems! I've committed a chapter to this issue at the end of this book.

If you are like most people, you have picked up this book hoping I will give you a few simple, magical suggestions that will transform your study overnight and make you a brilliant learner. Sorry, it's not that easy! Becoming a more exceptional learner still takes effort on your part. Don't give up on this book and look elsewhere for those secret shortcuts or, easy tricks to learning. Instead, optimize your learning by following the holistic, strategic approach outlined in this book, and identify the specific tactics that you can use to build a learning plan that helps you achieve your goals.

Let's get started.

References

Alter, A. L. (2013). The benefits of cognitive disfluency. *Current Directions in Psychological Science*, **22**(6), 437–442.

Ball, K., Berch, D. B., Helmers, K. F., Jobe, J. B., Leveck, M. D., Marsiske, M., . . . Tennstedt, S. L. (2002). Effects of cognitive training interventions with older adults: A randomized controlled trial. *Jama*, **288**(18), 2271-2281.

Diemand-Yauman, C., Oppenheimer, D. M., & Vaughan, E. B. (2011). Fortune favors the: Effects of disfluency on educational outcomes. *Cognition*, **118**(1), 114–118. doi:10.1016/j.cognition.2010.09.012

Chapter 1

The Holistic Learning Framework

Myth: All I need to improve my learning is to know a few quick study tricks.

Reality: There are many different powerful influences on learning. No single learning strategy will help everyone; instead, a comprehensive, strategic approach is required.

There is no doubt that great learners have to be smart and work hard. Those two features are indispensable, but are they enough to make a great learner and lead to a successful life? Face it, there will always be someone smarter or harder working than you. However, all is not lost.

If I needed to identify the most important feature of great learners, it is not about being super smart, or the hardest worker. Instead, I believe that the best learners are those who are strategic with their learning[1] (Ertmer & Newby, 1996). You need to be smart about your hard work. The best learners have convinced themselves that no matter how smart they are, they can always learn to learn better. They understand that optimal learning does

---
[1] Educators have long been advocating that learners should have a strategic approach to learning better, for decades in fact! They must know different learning strategies and be able to implement them into a plan. My goals for you after reading this book!

not come naturally, but requires proper thought and planning to achieve the goals that they want. Furthermore, they strategically implement what they have learned about learning.

Metacognition (thinking about thinking)

These strategic learners become experts in metacognition, which means "thinking about thinking." I call them experts because they naturally understand better than anyone else how they themselves personally learn. Now, I'm not saying that all of these learners need to spend lots of time considering all sorts of possibilities and writing out a learning plan in great detail. Some successful learners do that, but most don't. These learners often plan their learning strategy at an almost subconscious level. What all great learners have in common is that they learn more about how to learn, and then consider how they learn best. They implement new ideas on how they can learn and experiment with different methods of learning for different types of subjects. Finally, they evaluate how they actually learned, continuously improve their learning and revise and reset their plans when appropriate.

It is interesting to watch the reaction of some of our undergraduate students when they first learn how their classmates study for their classes. One of our first exercises in our Learning to Learn Better course is to ask students to share tips with each other about how they learn best. I find that some students are shocked to realize how strategic other students are with their studies. These surprised students have always just relied on their natural abilities to learn. They have never thought a moment *about* learning, and they've just done what ever felt right for them.

Until they heard what other students did, they never considered planning how to study.

They hadn't thought to schedule time to study for their examinations months ahead of time, and review shortly before the test. They didn't consider how they might pull together groups of other students to discuss and review the content of the course.

It is this approach — continuous trial and error followed by review and readjustment of study plans — that separates the best learners from ordinary ones. Indeed, there are many research studies which demonstrate that thinking about thinking, results in better learning and better academic success (Quigley, Muijs, & Stringer, 2018). Most of the students in our class are not struggling with their studies. Instead, they are looking for ways to improve their study techniques and better optimize their learning so as not to waste their precious time allocated for studying.

Some students report they had figured out for themselves many of the techniques that we teach in class. But they benefit from being reassured that what they are doing is supported by scientific research on learning.

Learning to learn better is an individual journey

There is no one specific reason why individuals struggle with their learning; and there many different ways in which you can improve your learning. And the techniques described in this book should be tailored for different disciplines. Your approach to the study of English literature may be quite different from your approach to that upper-division physics course.

I made the mistake of approaching my Japanese language class in college in the same way that I approached my biology courses. It was a disaster! Language classes were hard for me, and I did poorly, in part, because I didn't have a good learning strategy solidly in place. I didn't know enough at the time to plan more carefully for how to study for different subjects. And when my study strategy wasn't working, I didn't think to ask for help and try to change my plans. Instead, I just tried to work harder using my same study methods. But I soon ran up against such internal thoughts as: "you aren't very good at learning languages; you better give it up" and "learning another language isn't so important after all." These thoughts beat up any self-motivation I had to work harder. Instead, I needed to try a different approach to learning.

My experience working with and helping thousands of students over my career is that there is no one thing that keeps them from their peak academic success. It is overly optimistic to think that by merely changing a few study habits, there will be a substantial difference in their grades. Unfortunately, things are rarely so simple. There is always a multitude of issues that handicap their learning.

A holistic approach

Most books on learning focus on a few study techniques, with the idea that stringing these ideas together will improve learning. For example, if students mostly rely on rote memorization to do well in school, they suggest you will significantly benefit from techniques that deepen your knowledge and, as a result, forget things much slower.

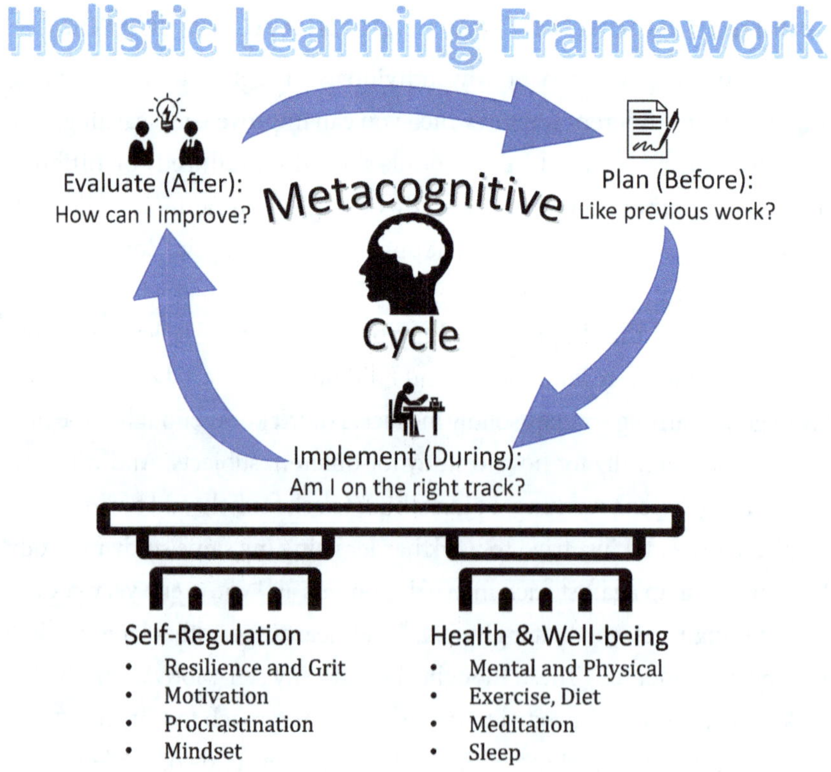

Holistic Learning Framework

Metacognitive Cycle
- Evaluate (After): How can I improve?
- Plan (Before): Like previous work?
- Implement (During): Am I on the right track?

Self-Regulation
- Resilience and Grit
- Motivation
- Procrastination
- Mindset

Health & Well-being
- Mental and Physical
- Exercise, Diet
- Meditation
- Sleep

Figure 1. The Holistic Learning Framework: A strategic approach to learning. Use the copy of this framework in Appendix A to keep track of the ideas you would like to incorporate into your learning plan.

The Holistic Learning Framework

Instead, I believe you need to adopt a more comprehensive or holistic approach to learning that recognizes that there are many influences that can impact learning. Since a picture is worth a thousand words, especially when it comes to trying to remember something, I have created a visual framework to help you keep track of the different areas that impact on your learning.

Use this drawing as a road map to help you organize what you learn in this book. Hopefully, it will encourage you to consider incorporating different aspects of learning into your plans.

The Holistic Learning Framework consists of two major parts. The upper part depicts a continuous cycle which involves setting goals for your studies, then planning and implementing your study plans, followed by reviewing and revising your plans. Then you start the process over again.

This part of the framework is known in the scientific literature as the Metacognitive Cycle (Tanner, 2012; Zimmerman, 2002). The image of a repeating sequence emphasizes that even after you have done the initial work of learning about learning and developing a study plan aligned with your personal academic goals, your job is not over. Students with great intentions put together a plan for their studies, but, after trying it out, fail to sit back for a moment and seriously reflect on whether their plan worked or not. This reflection and adjustment of their strategy is even more critical than selecting the right way to study to begin with.

This continuous cycle starts with setting useful goals. I have found that almost all students set learning goals. Unfortunately, for most, it is a wasted effort. The week before we discuss goal setting in class, we ask the students to write down a few learning goals. When we ask the students the following week if they achieved any of those goals, we find many had forgotten about them entirely. What seems easy and natural to do is actually complicated to do well.

The planning stage of the cycle doesn't just involve proper goal setting. After setting useful goals, it is critical to have a toolbox of strategies to attain those goals. As I previously mentioned, what makes implementing these strategies difficult is that we tend not to understand which strategies work best for us. Our natural inclination is to misjudge the value of the various learning techniques and strategies we use to reach those goals. Our learning myths get in the way of optimal learning.

And, importantly, it doesn't just stop there. During the second part of the cycle when you are implementing your plan, you should be monitoring how you are doing at the same time. You don't have to decide at this stage if your plans are working or not. It isn't the right time to try to change anything. Instead, you'd want to give your plans a chance to get established.

In the third part of the cycle, you evaluate how you have done. What are the areas that worked for you? How did you do with implementing your plan? Were there things that were harder for you to implement than you first thought? Did your plan achieve the goals you intended? How would you revise those plans? (Maybe the issue was not with the plan you came up with, but with your goals!)

After you have honestly reflected on the results of your learning plan, then you can begin to decide what areas merit adjusting. Even if you have achieved all of your goals, I suggest taking the attitude that there is always something to improve or make more efficient.

The new plan can be minor tweaks or major revisions. Then you start over again with the cycle. In subsequent chapters, we'll go into more detail about how to set goals that really work for you. We'll cover a variety of different techniques to use in your study plan. Then we'll help you monitor your implementation and then review and reset your plans. These steps compose the Metacognitive Cycle of our learning framework.

When I first started working with students to help them learn better, I found many of their study plans were simply "I'll figure it out as I go." These students were especially susceptible to falling for many of the learning myths presented in this book. For many of these students, getting them to develop their own, personalized Metacognitive Cycle using different learning strategies provided them the help that they most needed. Their learning was improved because they were previously unaware of the best methods for them to prepare for their studies. When learning didn't go well for them, they looked at different areas they could change instead of just deciding they didn't work hard enough.

The Holistic Learning Framework

> Writing my Learning Plan made me realize that I have always been making very general and broad goals. This often made me lose track and focus as I would find difficulty in tracking how much progress I was making. By setting short and specific goals or checkpoints, I am constantly able to ensure that I stay in check in terms of time and objectives.

Student, Year 3, NUS Faculty of Science

Knowing the best way to learn is not enough

However, for some students, the Metacognitive Cycle doesn't cover their most pressing issues. Over my career, I've had the opportunity to work with many bright students. Despite their intelligence and previous academic success, and their understanding of key learning strategies, some of these students were still not learning as well as they should. What were we missing?

I think it was my physician training that gave me the realization that teaching students about the Metacognitive Cycle did not provide them the complete picture. Just knowing how to study did not mean that students could implement their plans. I didn't see this at first because it was too obvious: If you don't have the self-discipline to get yourself to crack open the book and begin studying in the first place, you won't learn. If being in good health or a state of mind to study aren't properly in place, it won't make a difference what study techniques you choose. You won't be able to learn well if you feel sick or emotionally troubled. All students need a complete approach to better learning. Otherwise, they will not be able to implement what they learn.

Therefore, the bottom half of the framework represents the solid foundation necessary to create optimal learning. While the necessity of having this solid foundation may be obvious, what is surprising to me is that few students really know much about these factors and have these aspects solidly in place. For example, very few have any idea of the impact that their poor sleep habits have on their learning. The effect of sleep on learning is just one example of how we typically poorly understand how our brains work for optimal learning.

Chapter 1

Social determinants of learning

My experiences working with teachers struggling to figure out how to help their students made me realize that a holistic approach to learning does not stop with just these two foundational pillars either. I found that teachers sometimes fail to realize the real reason why their students aren't performing well in school. It might not necessarily be because they aren't motivated, or they lack the study techniques I describe in this book. For example, it may instead be that their home environment is unsupportive of education. This means, as I stated earlier, a more holistic approach to helping them succeed in school must be considered.

I won't address how the Holistic Learning Framework is affected by ubiquitous socio-economic/cultural factors that all students experience, but this is not because I believe they aren't important. Indeed, these social determinants of learning are extraordinarily powerful. For example, I think the attitudes of Asian societies towards the importance education has in one's future success is one of the key factors why many countries in Asia top the charts in the Organization of Economic Development (OECD) ranking of education systems around the world (Schleicher, 2019). I recently read a news story that mentioned an amazing fact: In 2019, half of all the perfect scores in the world on the International Baccalaureate examination came from Singaporean students (Ang, 2020). In Singapore, high achievement in education is greatly prized. To me, the cultural orientation to the importance of learning is the fundamental driver of such educational success.

In the same fashion, these social determinants of learning have the potential to significantly harm our students' ability to learn. The Economist Intelligence Unit ranked Singapore and the United States as two of the most food-secure countries in the world. Nevertheless, it is still estimated that upwards of 23,000 Singaporean children are malnourished.[2] In the United States, approximately one in seven students come from a household living

---

[2] Even in two of the richest and most food-secure counties in the world, there is still hunger. This problem is often hidden from our view. See https://foodsecurityindex.eiu.com/Index (https://www.nokidhungry.org/who-we-are/hunger-facts and https://borgenproject.org/top-10-facts-about-hunger-in-singapore/.

below the federal poverty level and begins each day at school hungry. If this occurs even in the two most food-secure countries in the world, what is happening in the rest of the world?

I don't think it takes much to convince you that poverty, homelessness or living in a crime-ridden or war-torn area of the world will diminish a student's ability to learn well. Taking on solutions to these problems are well beyond the scope of this book. While I won't cover these barriers to learning in this book, I mention this as a reminder that these social determinants of learning also have a significant impact.

Instead, we will focus our attention on the areas directly covered within the Holistic Learning Framework. Even with this much narrower scope, there is much to talk about and for you to figure out for yourself. There are many factors, such as your individual learning strengths and weakness, the discipline you are studying, and your personal learning goals, to take into account.

We will start our learning journey in the next chapter by going in depth on the top part of our Holistic Learning Framework: the Metacognitive Cycle and how this cycle should begin to shape your approach to learning better.

Summary: Chapter 1

Every learner is different and needs a personalized approach to learning better. Since there are so many different factors that can influence learning, a comprehensive approach is required. Strategic learners can use a holistic framework to organize themselves and develop their own learning plan.

References

Ang, J. (2020). Singapore IB students make up half of world's perfect scorers. *Straits Times,* Jan 4. Retrieved from https://www.straitstimes.com/singapore/education/spore-ib-students-make-up-half-of-worlds-perfect-scorers.

Ertmer, P. A., & Newby, T. J. (1996). The expert learner: Strategic, self-regulated, and reflective. *Instructional Science,* **24**(1), 1–24.

Quigley, A., Muijs, D., & Stringer, E. (2018). Metacognition and self-regulated learning: Guidance report. Education Endowment Foundation: UK.

Schleicher, A. (2019). PISA 2018: Insights and Interpretations. *OECD Publishing*.

Tanner, K. D. (2012). Promoting student metacognition. *CBE — Life Sciences Education,* **11**(2), 113–120.

Zimmerman, B. J. (2002). Becoming a self-regulated learner: An overview. *Theory into Practice,* **41**(2), 64–70.

Chapter 2

Setting Goals

Myth: Since so few people make and successfully achieve their goals, it can't be that important to do. I'll just do whatever comes up and not overthink it.

Reality: We all have goals that we follow whether we realize it or not. We should think more carefully about them.

Millions of people wake up each year in the fog of their late-night New Year's Eve celebration and, while half asleep, try to come up with their most important goal(s) for the year.

We see gyms in January bursting with people all vowing to be healthier and lose weight. However, a few months later, like clockwork, the crowds thin out and these same folks no longer find the time to work out. People with other types of goals (like eating more vegetables, getting more sleep or writing a book!) find themselves in a similar situation. We intrinsically understand that it makes sense for us to have goals in our lives. But most of our goals are useless because it is so hard for us to change.

So, why is it that we can't seem to have goals for ourselves that last beyond a few moments of wishful thinking? And if learning is so important to us, shouldn't we have goals that are focused on it?

Goal Setting Activity
(Approximate Duration: 2 minutes)
URL: www.strategiclearn.org
(go to Activities/Goal Setting)

Goals

Aim: Think about your goals.

Instructions: Select all of the goals (can select more than one) that are your most important goals.

We typically make our New Year's resolutions on the spur of the moment, without much thought. And while it seems natural to make these spontaneous goals, we don't know how to make goals that are worthwhile for us.

That is much harder work.

Setting more thoughtful goals

When my students say they don't set goals, what they are really saying is that they haven't seriously thought about their "true" goals. They might spend only a few minutes each year thinking about these goals. The reality is that even if they haven't thought very carefully about their goals, they still have them, but they aren't well-formed. As we live our lives and have to make decisions about how we spend our time, like it or not, they reflect our goals; whether they have been thoughtfully considered or not. Proper goal setting is the necessary first step of any strategic learning plan.

The vast majority of my students make goals, but they usually characterize generic goals that everyone else has: "I want to be healthier this year!" These goals are so vague that it is impossible to know how to go

Setting Goals

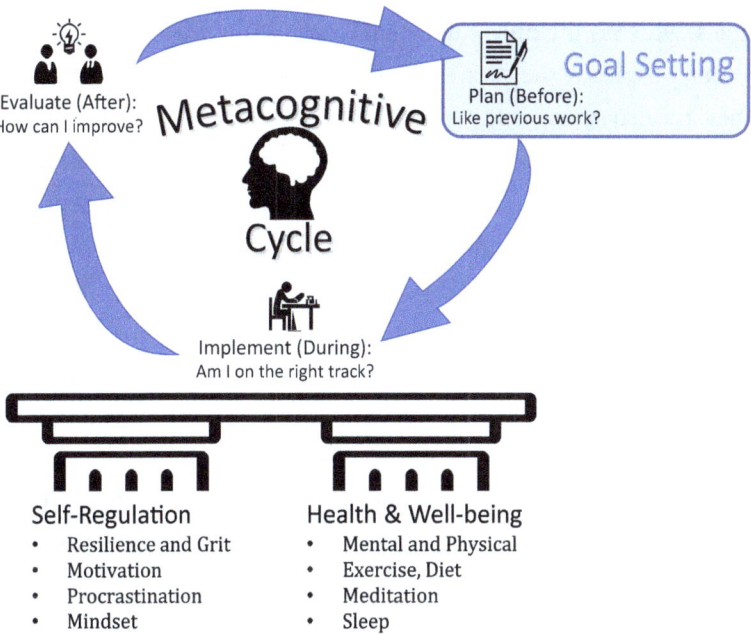

Figure 1. The Holistic Learning Framework: Learning Strategies. Goal setting is the first step of the Metacognitive Cycle.

about them or whether you have achieved them or not. These types of goals are usually not genuinely tailored for us. And when our goals don't reflect what we truly want, it is little wonder we find it hard motivating ourselves to do the work necessary to succeed with these goals.

When I give my students the above goal setting activity, they almost always say that all or most of those listed goals are important. And they might tell me other goals that are important to them as well. Unfortunately, when you select a large number of goals as important, it is the same as if you have chosen none of them as important.

Once we figure out what our most important goals are, then we face an even bigger problem: indecision with prioritizing our goals. Some of our goals might conflict with each other. My students often note that relaxing with friends conflicts with their goal of getting good grades at school. While this might not be entirely true (see Chapter 8: Health and Wellness, where

Chapter 2

I make the case that living a balanced life will improve learning), we need to understand which trade-offs we are willing to accept. Of these conflicting goals, which is the most important to you and under what circumstances? When people say they don't have the time to "eat well or exercise, etc." what they are also saying is those activities are not priority goals for them.[1]

Whether we realize it or not, whether or not we have thoughtfully considered our goals, we are forced to make choices concerning what we do with our time. Since none of us has more than a 24-hour day, we have to prioritize what we do. But if you are like most of us, the choices you make with your time do not always represent the choices you truly want to make. They may reflect what is easiest to do at the time, someone else's goals (like your parents'), or what you believe society expects from you.[2]

It is no wonder that most people try not to think too carefully about their goals; it can be overwhelming. But how can we possibly make the right decisions where to spend our precious time when we don't have a firm sense of our priorities?

Our brains are programmed to try to find the easy way out, rather than to expend energy to think about things more carefully. So, instead of taking on proper goal setting, we talk ourselves into the idea that making goals isn't necessary. But without doing the hard work of setting our goals, we just "wing it" or let whatever is most comfortable or most pressing at the time make our decisions for us. Doesn't it make sense to try to be more thoughtful about our goals?

---

[1] One of the biggest challenges my students complain about, especially my medical students, is the struggle for "work/life balance." However, this struggle (typically between demands of the job and demands on our time for family and friends) reflects our effort to figure out our priority life goals. Your friends and family may need to understand your goals and priorities as much as you. Their misunderstandings about your goals will lead to even more conflict than disagreements about your goals.

[2] You may have heard the term "tiger parent," a caricature view of an overly strict, demanding mom or dad. (Chua, 2011) The high value placed on education, high academic standard-setting, hard work, strong family values promoted by tiger parents is an integral part of Asian culture. The attention placed by parents on their children helps them attain success in their future careers. However, I see this parenting approach as a "Goldilocks" problem, as discussed later in this chapter. Too much of this tactic can be harmful psychologically to some children. It has to be "just right" for each child. And, no matter what goals our parents give us as young children, as we grow older, we must establish our own goals. Many times, our goals are aligned to our parents', but they need not necessarily be so.

How to make SMART goals

If setting goals were easy to do, then more people would make them and keep them.

When I first started to teach students how to make goals, we showed them a common method, known as SMART goals (Lawlor, 2012)[3]:

- (S)pecific: Is your goal clearly defined and not vague?
- (M)easurable: Can you measure the criteria to follow your progress?
- (A)chievable: Is the goal attainable for you?
- (R)elevant: Is the goal aligned with what you want?
- (T)ime-based: Is there a reasonable, defined time to achieve/measure this goal?

I found that the SMART format is useful for students just starting to learn how to make helpful goals. While I won't get into a debate here regarding the difference between a goal and an objective, let's just say that it is a common mistake to make our goals too vague to be useful. So, they become "non-goals" that anyone can reach depending on how they are defined.

For example, a goal of reading your textbook each day could mean just the first page of the chapter or it could mean the entire book. It could mean a light skimming of the material or an in-depth, concentrated reading and analysis. If your goals aren't defined clearly, then you can move them around until they are meaningless. Follow these SMART goal rules, and you will avoid some of these pitfalls.

Another tendency of our students is to make SMART goals that are outcomes of their effort, like getting straight As or winning a gold medal in the upcoming swimming meet. Outcomes can depend on many factors outside your control (for example, you could find yourself in the same swimming race with Gold Medal Olympians Michael Phelps and Joseph Schooling!). Instead, we suggest that our students make SMART goals around tasks instead of results: such as going to swimming practice twice a

---

[3] "SMART" as a method to develop business goals was first described in the literature by D.T. Doran in 1981. There have subsequently been many different published variations of SMART goals, with the letters representing different words that emphasize various features of goals. Lawlor's referenced paper described how to apply SMART goals to learning.

day for one hour. It is much more straightforward to monitor your progress towards tasks rather than outcomes.

A "not so" SMART (**S**pecific, **M**easurable, **A**chievable, **R**elevant and **T**ime-based) goal compared to a SMART goal

	A "not so" SMART goal: Get better grades in my Physics class next semester.	A SMART goal: Take a practice Physics exam for one hour each week during the course which tests my knowledge and get at least 80% correct.
Specific	This goal is not specific, i.e., how will you accomplish getting better grades?	This goal names a specific activity and time spent on this task.
Measurable	How much better grades do you seek? Does this apply to your final examination or course grade?	Clear, measurable specific goals of achievement, including both time spent and level of performance.
Achievable	Is this achievable? Or is this just wishful thinking?	It is reasonable to set aside one hour of your total study time to take a practice test each week. And you can study further if you are not geeting 80% correct
Relevant	This goal is relevant depending on your Aspirational goals. (see next section)	This goal is relevant depending on your Aspirational goals. (see next section)
Time-based	Does this goal refer to any moment of time in the semester? The timing stated is vague.	The amount of time spent and when this exam should be done is clearly set.

SMART goals are not enough: Aspirational Goals

As I taught our students how to set goals truly useful for them, I realized that setting goals was more complicated than just forming a few SMART goals.

While I think the SMART goal setting technique is quite helpful, at the same time, I find these SMART goals to be incomplete for most students. For example, many of our students have quite lofty and ambitious goals (like becoming a doctor or lawyer, winning a gold medal in the Olympics or owning their own company) that may or may not be achievable over any specific time. Should you ignore these big picture goals for things that are more task-oriented, short-term and achievable? I think not.

As a personal example, I set a specific amount of time each day to write this book. But probably more important to me is the big goal I have for this book: that it becomes a popular bestseller. Is that goal Specific? (Not really… What is the definition of a bestseller? If my mom buys a copy?) Is it Measurable? (Perhaps I could define the exact number of books sold for it to be a bestseller.) Is it Achievable? (Hopefully, but won't be easy.) Is it Relevant? (Yes) Is it Timely? (For this goal, I'll be incredibly happy and relieved if the book gets published, rather than for it to hit a specific deadline.)

I found it helpful for me to have ambitious intentions for my book as I was writing it. However, I was not ready to determine how many copies I should sell, over what period, or exactly which international bestseller list the book should get on. We distinguish these great big and often daring goals from SMART goals, calling them "aspirational goals." My aspirational goal of writing a book was motivating for me and what I needed at the time. Useful aspirational goals are just beyond our typical reach. They should be as big and audacious as you can muster, but don't let them be so big as to create so much fear it demotivates you. These are the goals that allow you to stand out from the crowd; potentially unachievable, but still believable to you.

Both aspirational and SMART goals are needed. Align your short-term SMART goals with those longer-term aspirational goals. Your SMART goals are the steps that lead you towards reaching your aspirational goals. I can

Chapter 2

monitor my progress using my SMART goals, and that helps me keep on track. But keeping my aspirational goals in mind makes it easier to make those tough decisions prioritizing what I should or should not do with my time.

Setting your aspirational goals

When I ask our students for their main aspirational goals, they typically respond with things like "straight As" or becoming a multi-millionaire. However, I'm not necessarily suggesting that aspirational goals are just career or academic ambitions, such as starting a non-profit to save the environment, becoming a professional basketball star or university professor. I encourage them instead to think from a broader set of categories which include close relationships with family and friends, or optimizing their health, or fulfilling spiritual goals. Again, we all have these goals in our heads, whether or not

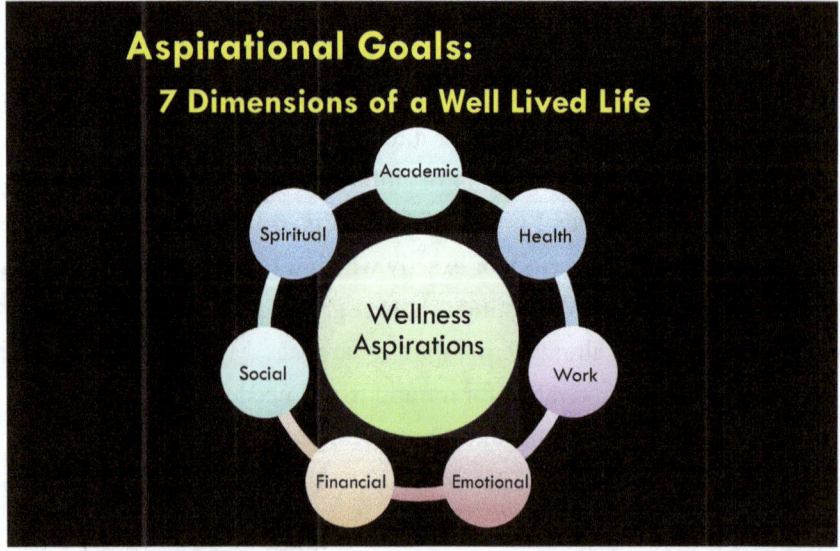

Figure 2. Seven Dimensions of a Well-lived Life: Other considerations to value.[4]

---

[4] There are many different versions of models that describe the dimensions that contribute to personal wellness. I have adapted these models to come up with what I believe represents the seven most essential dimensions to living a "well-lived life."

Setting Goals

Aspirational Goals:
7 Dimensions of a Well Lived Life

- Academic: Learning new skills and knowledge, being creative
- Health: Medical therapy, proper eating, exercise practice
- Work: Fulfillment and satisfaction with your career
- Emotional: Understanding and coping with your feelings
- Financial: Freedom from worry about finances
- Social: Understanding and positive relationships with others
- Spiritual: Developing sense of meaning in life

Figure 2. (*Continued*)

we have formalized them in our daily practice. Wouldn't it be helpful to be clearer on the aspirational goals that are most meaningful to you?

These seven dimensions represent aspects that should be evaluated by anyone considering how to achieve a "well-lived life." These dimensions are connected in the figure because some of your goals will affect more than one dimension. Use this model to help you consider and decide on your aspirational goals. There will be times during your life when one aspect needs more attention than another. For example, while in school, most students prioritize their academic/intellectual development over their satisfaction with their current financial situation. However, we should re-evaluate our aspirational goals and change our focus from time to time. Setting a new direction in our life means committing to new aspirational goals. These new goals, in turn, guide us on how to use our time.

I considered writing a book for many years but could never get started on it. I found it challenging to find the time and energy to write because I prioritized my leadership work in the university. These roles required heavy demands on my time, and along with my other aspirational goals, made it impractical to set any writing goals. I didn't need to get mad at myself for not working on the book; the timing wasn't right. However, once I had decided to set writing this book as one of my main aspirational goals, I decided I had to change from full-time to part-time work to accommodate that goal. That job change required a significant financial adjustment, but the need to make that decision was clear when I finally committed to my aspirational goal of writing this book.[5]

Writing this book is another personal example of how difficult it can be to set the right goals for oneself. I'm not a natural writer and taking words from my brain and moving them to my laptop can be painful at times. Typically, after writing for an hour or so, I am exhausted. How do I motivate myself to sit down in front of my computer, ignore the myriad of other top items on my "to-do" list, and write for a couple of hours each morning? Once I decided that it was the right time to pursue my aspirational goal of writing this book, my motivations to reach for this goal were aligned and clear to me.

Goldilocks and getting things "just right"

The other aspect which makes setting SMART goals so tricky and potentially discouraging is that they have what I call the "Goldilocks and the Three Bears" problem. For those of you who don't know the story, Goldilocks and the Three Bears is a 19th-century children's fairy tale, where a young girl named Goldilocks is wandering in a forest and happens upon a house owned by the three bears: Papa, Mama and Baby Bear. The bears aren't home, so Goldilocks decides to enter the house. She finds three meals on the table; one is too hot and the next is too cold, but she finally eats the one (Baby Bear's) that is "just right." Similarly, she finds one of the chairs (Baby Bear's) "just the right size" but she breaks it after sitting in it. Tired, she goes upstairs to try different beds and eventually finds one of the beds (Baby Bear's again) "just right" to fall asleep in. The bears eventually came home to find their food eaten

---

[5] If you are struggling with deciding on your aspirational goals, you can try this idea. Go ahead and write your own obituary. It doesn't matter whether you try to write an accurate account of your life or something that represents a life you wished you had. If you choose to write a true statement, you should ask yourself if this is how you want people to remember you. If it is a fictional account, you should ask if you are doing anything to achieve it. Either way, you should now have a better idea of the aspirational goals that are important to you.

Setting Goals

Figure 3. Goldilocks and the Three Bears: Getting things just right, otherwise… trouble!
Source: https://commons.wikimedia.org/wiki/File:Goldilocks_1912.jpg

and their furniture broken. They then discover Goldilocks in Baby Bear's bed. Hearing the bears come in, Goldilocks wakes up from her sleep with a shriek and then runs out of the house never to return. (The actual story is much more entertaining than my version, but I think you get the picture.)

We already defined SMART goals as being not so hard as to be unachievable. At the same time, if goals are too easy, then they become meaningless and a waste of time to set. They need to be "just right."

Lev Vygotsky was a Russian learning theorist who coined the expression "zone of proximal development" (Vygotsky, 1980). Vygotsky theorized that to learn optimally, we need to be in this zone, where learning is possible with the right amount of assistance. If the material is too difficult, we get overwhelmed or discouraged and stop learning. And if we find things too easy to learn, we don't progress with gaining new knowledge either. Everyone has their own zone of proximal development.

Proper goal setting is another instance of the need to find that optimal zone. Getting things "just right" also means getting things right for a moment in time. As time goes by, we get more skilled at a task. Goals that were previously "just right" can quickly become too easy as we learn more about a subject. But how do students possibly find that optimal zone for their goals?

Feedback

When scientists were first trying to engineer how to navigate their rockets to reach a particular target, they started by trying to calculate all of the factors that could influence how their missile flew through air and space. Given all of this information, they initially thought it possible to program the rocket at the launch with the right flight path that would reach their target. However, they found it was impossible to navigate the missile in this manner successfully.

They realized they could never know all of the factors that would come up that could change the flight pattern of the rocket. There were too many unanticipated factors not under their control (such as a last-minute change in the weather). They eventually figured out how to navigate the missile by using the idea of "feedback." They designed their rocket to monitor its location in space and the relation of that position to wherever they wanted it to go. Whenever the rocket started to drift off course, whatever the reason, they used that information to "feedback" to the rocket engines so the rocket could compensate and get itself back on the right path.

The expression "this isn't rocket science" is typically meant to reflect a situation that isn't so intellectually challenging. Well, to me, goal setting is indeed rocket science, and while it seems easy enough to do, it is difficult to do well. And rocket science can help us set goals better.

Most people who set goals don't follow through with them. Their problem isn't with setting goals in the first place. Instead, their problem is expecting that goal setting should be easier to do. Your first goals are likely to be wrong and need to be reconsidered, readjusted to your current situation and then reset. While we shouldn't readjust our goals so frequently that they become meaningless, they must be kept in the "just right" zone. Similarly, we teach goal setting to our students to reflect this continually changing nature of the path toward their long-term goals. We should not be discouraged when we don't reach our immediate SMART goals.

Our SMART goals can tell us when we've shot for too high or too difficult a target. In that case, we need to change our expectations to something more realistic. In contrast, if we have too easily reached our goals, then it is time to reflect more on them and make them more challenging. We should expect to continuously adjust our goals depending on how we are doing, just like a rocket does to reach its target.

Goals must be adjusted to be "just right"

People approach goals as a fixed target that shouldn't change — they have an image of the goal posts in soccer or the goal line in American football. These stationary targets remain the same no matter what happens, and we must find a way to make that goal to score points.

For some goals, like getting better grades or losing weight, having a target in mind is useful to monitor your progress and keep yourself moving toward the goal. However, for many, once they achieve those goals, they can slip back, unable to maintain that target. For example, although a startling two-thirds of Americans are overweight, only one in six has lost weight and maintained that weight loss. (Kraschnewski *et al.*, 2010). For many of those who have briefly lost weight and slipped back, somewhere in their minds, they believe they have reached their goals and can now relax. For these types of goals, changing the metaphor from a destination (reaching a certain weight) to a journey (the lifelong pursuit of having good health) is helpful not only to reach their goals but to maintain them (Huang & Aaker, 2019).

We encourage our students to get started with goal setting and then continually adjust to the changing, often unanticipated nature of life. When we try hard and don't hit our targets, we should quickly forgive ourselves and just learn from what happened. Perhaps our strategies to achieve those goals weren't right. Or the goals themselves weren't quite right.

Chapter 2

While coming up with any old goal is easy for us to do, defining the goals that are helpful to us is different and quite challenging. It should come as little surprise that even a few weeks or months after setting goals, most people have not started on or even remembered them. And of those who actually started to pursue their goals, few continue. Just like other aspects of learning where "hard work" is necessary to make actual progress, properly setting goals requires a considerable amount of thought and reflection.

So, how do your learning goals fit in with the other important goals in your life? Get started by naming a couple of aspirational goals and list a few aligned SMART goals. And once you have a set of goals useful to you, evolve those goals over time to keep them "just right." Pay attention when your goal-setting influences a decision you make with how you use your time. For example, were you OK with your decision to turn down your friend's invitation to hang out so that you could study for that upcoming exam? If not, then perhaps your learning goals are set incorrectly. Think about how you spend the majority of your time. (Yes, even think about the amount of time that you sleep each day!) Perhaps you need to reconsider your aspirational goals. Your goals and the priorities you set for them should be consistent with the time you spend on them.

Reflecting on your goals is vital to fine-tune what you genuinely want. Only you can do that work. Now, let's start to build the strategies that you can employ to reach your learning goals.

> *Right now, I have my SMART goals with me, pasted on my physical calendar at home where I am able to see it. I believe that if I can see it in my room every day, I will stick better to it and remember that I have to adhere to these SMART goals. This applies to my new studying techniques...I have printed out the advice to see it everyday too.*

Student, Year 4, NUS Faculty of Science, Chemistry

Summary: Chapter 2

Every strategic learner should start by making and prioritizing aspirational and SMART goals. These serve as the basis for your learning plan. These goals should evolve over time and will need adjusting to stay "just right" for you.

References

Chua, A. (2011). *Battle Hymn of the Tiger Mother.* Bloomsbury Publishing: London.

Huang, S.-C., & Aaker, J. (2019). It's the journey, not the destination: How metaphor drives growth after goal attainment. *Journal of Personality and Social Psychology,* **117**(4), 697–720.

Kraschnewski, J., Boan, J., Esposito, J., Sherwood, N. E., Lehman, E. B., Kephart, D. K., & Sciamanna, C. (2010). Long-term weight loss maintenance in the United States. *International Journal of Obesity,* **34**(11), 1644–1654.

Lawlor, K. B. (2012). *Smart goals: How the application of smart goals can contribute to achievement of student learning outcomes.* Paper presented at the Developments in Business Simulation and Experiential Learning: Proceedings of the Annual ABSEL Conference.

Chapter 3

The Metacognitive Cycle — Recognition vs Recall

Myth: I know when I know something and when I don't remember it.

Reality: The difference between recognizing something and being able to recall it is not obvious, and there is only one way to know the difference (read this chapter to find out).

The Metacognitive Cycle is the top part of the Holistic Learning Framework and is the engine of any successful learning plan. As we learned from the last chapter, our cycle starts with our Plan, which includes an understanding of our personal goals and how our learning goals fit in with all of the other important goals in our lives. We have described both SMART and aspirational goals and getting them connected and "just right." The Plan part of the Metacognitive Cycle not only includes your learning goals but also incorporates different learning strategies to help you optimize your study and reach those goals.

We now turn to learning more about these strategies.

What surprises learners about the learning strategies used in the Metacognitive Cycle is that so many of them seem to defy our "common sense" ways of learning. The surprises begin with our sense of how well we are learning.

Chapter 3

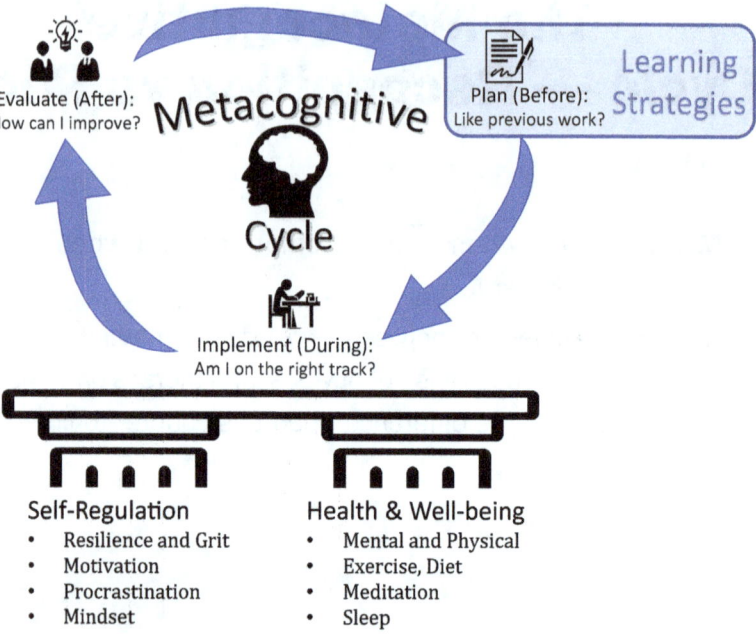

Figure 1. The Holistic Learning Framework: Incorporating learning strategies into our learning plan. These strategies are organized by the three features of how we forget.

If you are like many students, you believe that "you know what you know and know what you don't." You hold a few pieces of information in your short-term memory, and by studying, you can move this knowledge into long-term memory to remember for the upcoming test. You might stay up all night before the test, so you can cram as much as possible into your short-term memory, unloading that information for the exam. Unfortunately, these beliefs will keep you from optimizing your learning.

Why memorize anything?

In today's world, with the constant presence of a smartphone readily accessible to us, and availability of search engines that can seemingly answer any question, the value of remembering things just doesn't seem the same as it used to be. Information is everywhere, and with each passing day, it is becoming even more effortless to obtain. Some educators have wondered if it is even necessary to remember anything these days. This opinion is similar to one that was sounded in the past when many felt that using a calculator in class would allow mathematics learners to spend their mental energies on more complex problems. Reassuringly, the use of calculators has not resulted in generations of learners unable to multiply, divide or perform other simple calculations.

Given the technology currently available to us, searching on the internet for information has become an arguably more vital skill to have than a great rote memory. After first finding a variety of different possible answers via an online search, we must then develop the more challenging ability to critically analyze what we have found: deciding whether the material is relevant to our question, whether or not the information is credible, etc. This critical thinking skill is one of the most important "twenty-first-century" skills.

Nevertheless, I would still argue that without any basic set of facts that can be easily recalled (memorized), there isn't enough information in our brains to think critically about and be creative with.[1] It would be inefficient to stop each time to look up frequently needed information. We are usually better off spending our time looking up infrequently used but critically important information than relying on our too often flawed memory. While I recognize there is a continuing debate on how much we should memorize versus how much we should rely on technology, I think it is safe to say that some memorization of information is required and optimizing this skill is still important. At the very least, for most of the readers of this book, memorization is still quite important to successfully perform in school examinations.

Unfortunately, the real story about memory is not quite so simple, especially when it comes to learning. To give you a better sense of how complicated this is, let's begin with the following exercise as a starting point for understanding more about our memory.

---

[1] For those who want to read more about the debate about memorization and thinking, I recommend the book, "Why Don't Students Like School?" by D.T. Willingham. He has the enviable ability to turn scientific findings on human cognition into sensible arguments about education (Willingham, 2009).

Day at the Zoo Activity
(Approximate Duration: 5–7 minutes Over a 20 minute time period)
URL: www.strategiclearn.org

Zoo

Aim: Understand the difference between Recognition and Recall. Even if you are trying to skim through this book as quickly as possible, I highly recommend this particular activity.

Instructions: This activity involves two parts: the first is watching a video. Please wait at least 15 minutes or longer before doing the second part. The activity won't work as well if you don't. You are free to do anything during this fifteen-minute-break.

You will need to have a way to write a few words down (paper/pen or note app on your phone). While you are doing this exercise, rely on your memory only; don't take notes on what you see until you are instructed.

Recognition versus recall

Memory researchers have for years used the model of short- and long-term memory (and working memory) to pursue their investigations (Cowan, 2008). Short-term memory is when our brain learns something new, then allows us to mimic it back before quickly forgetting it. If we do certain things, such as study that information in depth, that portion of our short-term memory can enter long-term memory. The factual information stored in long-term memory then becomes accessible to us at a future date for use in exams, work, trivia contests, etc. Short-term memory is limited, the brain is only able to keep a small amount of material (sometimes stated as five to seven pieces of information) there at any point in time.[2] The definition of working memory in the literature varies, but it is generally considered to be where focused information is processed by the brain and then appropriately stored.

While this model has led researchers to better understand the science of memory, it doesn't fully reflect what I experience for myself when I'm learning. Factual memory is very dynamic and complex, not just the movement of some information that either goes from short-term memory to our long-term memory bank for permanent storage or is quickly forgotten. That model is closer to how a computer works, but I find it is not so helpful for my students trying to understand how they can learn better. Instead, my thoughts about my own long-term memory is that it tends to drift from something I can easily recall to something that remains only in my subconsciousness. Some memories will strongly last in my consciousness for the rest of my life, and others seem to last only a few seconds, never to come up again unless somehow triggered back.

When it comes to teaching students about learning, instead of asking them to classify their memories into the short- versus long-term model, we teach our students to understand the difference between recognition and recall. When we remember something, we recognize that we have experienced it before using our senses: we have seen, heard, felt, tasted or smelled it. Of all the things that we can recognize, we can quickly and freely recall only a portion.

In other words, recognition is the ability to determine whether or not you have previously seen or experienced something when presented with a reminder. Our long-term memory can store considerable amounts of information that we can recognize. Recall is the ability to remember something without additional clues or prompts; it is the ability to "retrieve" that fact or image from our memory. When you recognize someone that you met earlier but don't remember their name until they remind you, it is

---

[2] For purposes of this discussion and simplicity, I'm limiting this discussion to factual memory, which is only one of the knowledge types described in the revised Bloom's Taxonomy. The other types of knowledge identified in this publication are: conceptual, procedural and metacognitive (Krathwohl & Anderson, 2009).

precisely that difference that you are experiencing. When we pause in the middle of a speech as we desperately try to find the right word that escapes us, we recognize that the desired term exists in our brains but are again troubled by our inability to recall it. However, we could quickly resolve our memory lapse if presented with a variety of different words to choose from.

In the Day at the Zoo activity above, approximately 90% of our in-class students are plus or minus one away from remembering the correct number of new animals shown in the second video. However, very few could freely recall most of the animals they had seen in the first video. So, what does this mean? To detect this number of new animals in the second video correctly, they must have correctly recognized all or almost all of the animals in the first video, even though they weren't able to recall them. This is the difference between recognizing something they have seen before and being able to freely recall it.

While our brains have developed the ability to recognize vast amounts of information, our storage of "recallable" information is more limited. Internet search engines take advantage of this memory principle: They ask you first to recall a more easily retrievable keyword or idea. The search engine results page then provides a list of possible answers and websites for you to recognize and then choose the one you are interested in. Search engines understand you might not be able to exactly recall the right words to use in the search. All you need to do is get close enough and then recognize the ideas you were trying to find.

It is no wonder that students like multiple-choice questions (MCQ) over other formats that require recall, such as short answer or essay questions. They find it easier to ace an MCQ test because these questions usually test for recognition. And faculty prefer to assess students using MCQs because they are easier to grade, which is especially important for large classes of students. While it is possible to write an MCQ test that requires recall, it is more difficult and less frequently done. Unfortunately, real life problems, such as solving an issue facing your business, or engineering an innovative new design, will not typically present themselves with a list of solutions to recognize and select from. The primary point of education should be to prepare us for a life applying what we have learned to solve problems instead of recognizing different facts we have memorized.

Image recognition

Remarkably, our brain can effortlessly remember seeing thousands of images, even those observed only for a few seconds.[3] And our minds are well programmed to continue to recognize them for long periods. Yuval Noah Harari, in his book *Sapiens, A Brief History of Humankind*, makes the point that our brains have evolved from ancient hunter-gatherers. Our human ancestors needed to recognize thousands of different plants and animals. Edible or poisonous? Safe to eat and tasty, or dangerous and you might be eaten? Early man had little time to react, so, over time, we developed the ability not only to recognize tremendous amounts of information but to use this information to act quickly when required (Harari, 2014).

Harari makes the point that as human societies evolved into more complex civilizations, recognizing images was not enough. New types of information, such as numbers and data, became necessary. Unfortunately, our minds were not as well suited to keep this type of information in our memories, and what was remembered was lost after we died. It wasn't until the innovation of writing and documenting our knowledge that our societies were able to progress beyond small circles of individuals.

We collect billions of traces of memory that remain present in our brains, giving us the remarkable ability to recognize images we saw for the first time a long time ago. Nevertheless, our ability to recall those same images is much more limited. Another example of this difference comes from those who have learned another language early in life, only to later lose that ability from disuse. They no longer remember the words to express

---

[3] Psychologist Richard Wiseman asked two research assistants to look at thousands of images over a weekend. After seeing 10,000 images, they were able to recognize approximately 65% of them later! Although he named his experiment "Total Recall" (like the 1990 Arnold Schwarzenegger film), it would be more accurate to say he tested his assistants for the less catchy term: "Total Recognition". (http://www.richardwiseman.com/quirkology/new/USA/Experiment_totalRecall.shtml)

themselves. However, when these individuals try to learn that language again later in life, they can pick it up much more quickly, they can more effortlessly recognize the meaning of words and it is easier for them to speak with just the right accent. Some memory for speaking that language still exists, even if it feels like all is lost.

We think we can recall what we can recognize

The Day at the Zoo activity demonstrates that what our brain can recall is different from what it can recognize. When we say that we've forgotten something, we typically mean that we've lost the ability to recall it, but part or even all of it may still be in our brains. Both are different forms of "knowing" the material. It is hard for the brain to sort out what it can retrieve versus what it can only recognize, and the mind is surprised when the two aren't the same. We believe we should be able to recall anything we can recognize. A typical expressions of this difference is: "It was on the tip of my tongue, but I couldn't find the right word." We have all been there.

Forgetting is just human nature. Ironically, we find it easy to forget that we forget, even though we ALL experience forgetting first-hand, and it repeatedly happens to all of us. I still hear the surprise in the voices of students when they tell me that they studied the material, and thought they knew it, but couldn't remember it during the examination. Just as frequently, I hear from astonished faculty colleagues complaining when their students forget. They were surprised that the human anatomy that medical students learned during their first year in school could not be remembered the following year during their surgery rotation.

Learning requires retrieval of the right information at the right time and thinking about it in the right ways. Memory deals with just getting information to a place in our brain that can be actively processed further. During the stress of an exam, we want to make the information necessary to answer the test question as easily retrievable for our brains as possible. We optimize our learning by facilitating our ability to recall important information essential for answering those questions.

The Metacognitive Cycle — Recognition vs Recall

Our ability to recall information quickly fades over time, so what we can remember at one moment might not be available to us during the next. The only way to distinguish what the brain can retrieve (recall) from memory is to test it. And lucky for us, as we check ourselves to determine whether we know it well enough to recall, we reinforce (or practice) our ability to retrieve it from memory. When it comes to learning, studying a subject in much more depth will make that information and other information associated with it more easily "recallable." Less time spent on a topic or less efficient study of it will mean it requires more mental effort the next time we try to retrieve it.

So, recognizing something is easy work for our brains. It doesn't take much work at all to do. Recalling it is harder work. What are the learning strategies that we can use to help us remember and recall rather than just recognize things better? To improve how we study, these strategies should be incorporated into the "Plan" part of our Holistic Learning Framework.

The forgetting curve: 3 major features of how we remember and forget

The process of forgetting was systematically studied in the 1880s by Herman Ebbinghaus (1913). At a time when most researchers were trying to identify how people learned new information, he had the insight to measure instead

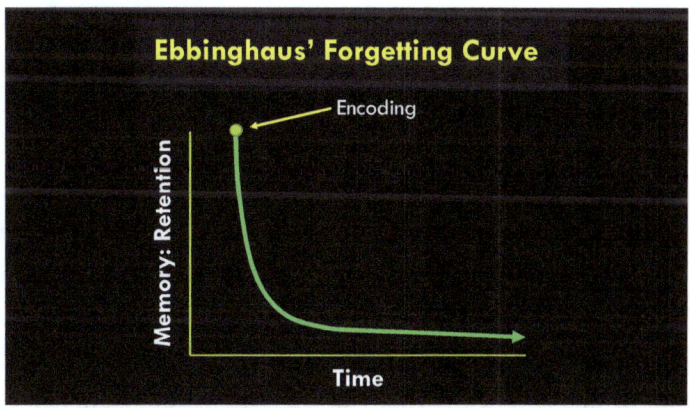

Figure 2.   Ebbinghaus' Forgetting Curve.

how people forgot what they had initially learned. In his classic experiments, he painstakingly studied how people forget. His research subject: himself! He memorized long lists of nonsensical words (consonant-vowel-consonant combinations, such as "GAD") and recorded how quickly he forgot them. Ebbinghaus meticulously performed his experiments; when his experiments were re-done 100 years later, remarkably, identical results were obtained (Murre & Dros, 2015)!

Ebbinghaus documented what we all experience: We take data from our five senses and place that information into our memory. This step is called encoding. And then, after it is in our memory, it very rapidly begins to go away.

In fact, when it came to his random letters, Ebbinghaus found that he forgot/could not recall over half of what he had learned after the first hour. The remaining facts then more slowly drifted away.

Ebbinghaus found three significant characteristics about forgetting:

- It is possible to enhance the initial encoding of information to improve memory.
- There are activities (learning strategies) that can subsequently be employed to slow the decay of forgetting and allow information to be retained for a longer time.
- Re-introducing the material at a later time resets the forgetting curve, quickly returning the memory of that information to a higher level.

For my students, I've organized how we can facilitate our memory into three categories, which reflect different features of Ebbinghaus' forgetting curve. For each of these categories, I'll describe the different learning strategies that influence memory retention. I admit my groupings are a bit of an over-simplification since many of these different categories interact and overlap with each other. But if you can forgive me for these somewhat fuzzy distinctions, I find it helps students better understand and retain how different learning strategies help their brains remember better.

1. The first aspect of memory that we can influence is encoding when our brains first encounter information to learn. These are things we can do prior to and while initially encoding this information.
2. The second feature of the curve we can influence comes immediately after we encode that information. As our memory rapidly begins to fade away, we can take actions that flatten the forgetting curve, so our memory of that material is more durable and retrievable.
3. The third feature of the forgetting curve is our ability to "reset" our memory after it fades. In other words, we can quickly "boost" our memory of that information after much of it has faded away. We can efficiently return our memory to the point when we first encountered and encoded that material.

We'll discuss how we can influence each of these aspects of the forgetting curve in the next three chapters.

Summary: Chapter 3

To learn and perform well on exams, students need to be able to recall, not just recognize information. Our brains are good at recognition. However, we typically lose our ability to recall information very quickly after learning it. The rate of forgetting can be altered by the learning strategies we incorporate into our learning plans.

References

Cowan, N. (2008). What are the differences between long-term, short-term, and working memory? *Progress in Brain Research, 169*, 323–338.

Ebbinghaus, H. (1913). *Memory* (H. A. Ruger & C. E. Bussenius, trans.). Teachers College: New York, 39.(Original work published 1885.)

Harari, Y. N. (2014). *Sapiens: A Brief History of Humankind*. Random House: UK.

Krathwohl, D. R., & Anderson, L. W. (2009). *A Taxonomy for Learning, Teaching, and Assessing: A Revision of Bloom's Taxonomy of Educational Objectives*: Longman.

Murre, J. M., & Dros, J. (2015). Replication and analysis of Ebbinghaus' forgetting curve. *PloS one*, **10**(7), https://doi.org/10.1371/journal.pone.0120644.

Willingham, D. T. (2009). *Why Don't Students Like School?: A Cognitive Scientist Answers Questions About How The Mind Works And What It Means For The Classroom*. John Wiley & Sons: New Jersey.

Chapter 4

The Metacognitive Cycle — Encoding Memory

Myth: Making memories is like taking photographs or videotaping a lecture.

Reality: Your brain actively edits what you remember and makes connections with other memories; you just don't realize it. You can use this feature of memory to study more effectively.

Your brain first takes in information using one of your senses (vision, hearing, taste, smell, touch), whether you are reading a book, watching a YouTube video or tasting coffee. It then processes that information into a more complex abstract thought that is stored and recalled later. This process is known as encoding. There are ways for us to better prepare our brains for this encoding process that results in retaining that memory longer. We'll examine this aspect of memory in this chapter.

What we usually don't recognize are the additional inputs from our senses and memory that come in at the same time we encode. These other inputs add and continue to associate with that new memory. Our prior knowledge and experiences influence how the brain encodes information, whether or not we are conscious of it. Furthermore, our brain edits out what it believes is not critical, and it can splice in materials from other memories; it can even imagine new things and add pieces to fill in the missing information.

All without us realizing it!

The Fa Da La Activity
(Approximate Duration: 5 minutes)

URL: www.strategiclearn.org
(go to Activities/Fa Da La)

Fa Da La

Aim: Demonstrate that the brain interprets our various sensory inputs while encoding. Memory is not like a simple recording of an event.

Instructions: Watch the video and select the sound that you hear.

Encoding memory

The mind is not just like a movie camera and doesn't merely record raw footage for memory to play back at a later time. Instead, our memory is like a fully edited feature film produced by our brains!

In the Fa Da La activity, the video shows me saying different words, while you are hearing the same audio track! However, our mind interprets and "hears" the sound depending on what it looks like I am saying. This video demonstrates what is known as the McGurk effect. Your perception of what you hear is surprisingly resistant to change: depending on what video you are looking at, you still hear different words even after knowing that the soundtrack is the same.

> **Pass the Ball Activity by Daniel J Simons**
> (Approximate Duration: 5–7 minutes)
> **URL: www.strategiclearn.org**
> (go to Activities/Pass the Ball)
> (Source: https://www.youtube.com/watch?v=IGQmdoK_ZfY)
>
>
> Pass the Ball
>
> **Aim:** Another interesting example of how the brain works while encoding memories.
>
> **Instructions:** Carefully watch the following YouTube video and count how many times the white team passes the ball to another player. Try hard to concentrate on getting the count correct. It isn't easy! If you are seeing this activity for the first time, please enter your numbers in our poll, otherwise leave blank.

This video demonstrates another remarkable example of how our minds naturally work, including tuning out (even quite dramatic) information. Less than half of our students who have seen this basketball video for the first time, see this game correctly!

At the same time as our brains are encoding what we see, it performs additional processing of our sensory inputs to form our memories of the basketball game. We don't realize what is filtered out or what else is included into our memories of the event. As a result, we are not always fully aware of the different connections our brains make or don't make when we encode the information learned for our classes.

However, as we encode information to our memory, are there things we can do to retrieve this information better later on? There are indeed individuals with remarkable memories and even international "Olympic" contests to determine champion memorizers. These extraordinary individuals can memorize such things as the New York City phone book in 23 minutes and repeat with 100 percent accuracy; an impressive feat that most of us would claim as a learning "super-power."

Joshua Foer's book *Walking with Einstein* features this particular group of individuals (Foer, 2012). He chronicles his journey into competing and eventually winning memorizing contests, even though he and many of the other contestants claim to possess only an average memory to start with. Foer's experience illustrates that the techniques used by these elite memorizers are not just available to a lucky few, naturally gifted individuals, but to anyone. Everyone can learn these skills, many of which rely on purposefully encoding familiar connections along with the new information they want to remember. All it seems to take is practice and a good strategy to encode the information.

The title of Foer's book is a bit misleading, however. Prodigious memory skill is different from the ability to think or create. Einstein reportedly even had trouble remembering his own phone number! And those who can memorize large amounts of information do not necessarily have the skills and insight to work out anything close to a Theory of Relativity. But these memory champions do have the ability to make quick connections with the information they have learned so that they can retrieve it in the future more easily.

Chunking information together

The most common way that people memorize large amounts of material during encoding is by having a system that allows them to associate it with smaller amounts of information that represent it. These smaller bits of information are less demanding to remember simply because there is less to remember. If this system is associated with things we already know well, the memory is even easier to retrieve. These associations could be objects, number patterns (like descending numbers starting from five), images, places or an infinite number of other possibilities. After remembering these smaller bits of information, they can be "decoded" when needed later to recall the full memory.

The Metacognitive Cycle — Encoding Memory

The most basic form of this technique is called "chunking," and we all use this principle to remember things. Take credit cards and phone numbers, which group numbers together. Remembering a phone number: 9738-5007 is much easier for us to picture in our minds and remember than one long string of individual digits: 9-7-3-8-5-0-0-7. Phone numbers are even easier to remember because some of the chunks represent different areas of the world (country and state area codes) that we share with many of our family and friends. We already know those chunks of numbers well.

Remembering other items using chunking is common as well. For example, medical students usually remember bones in the body by chunking them by location (bones of the palm versus the fingers of the hand) first. When you need to memorize something, consider how to group it in a way that is logical for you. The mere act of thinking about how to logically (at least to you!) group things will also help keep the information more retrievable to you.

Mnemonics and other associations

It is very helpful to chunk information into bits that can be associated with other easily recalled memories.

For example, the last four digits of my childhood phone number are 7412, and as a result, these numbers are firmly planted in my memory. If I'm lucky enough to need to remember that particular number sequence (or even a number close to that pattern) for another reason, I remember it by visualizing the telephone used in the house I grew up in. If I need to remember the number pattern "808," I just picture myself because I associate the number "808" with my first name: "BOB." For me, associating a number with an image that I know well helps me keep those numbers in my memory longer.[1]

---

[1] If the encoding information is more relatable or associated with yourself in some way, it is even more effective (self-reference effect). Semantic encoding is when the meaning of the information is encoded rather than the sound or image of it.

Chapter 4

The association of information with images is an example of a mnemonics and is another technique commonly used for memory. Mnemonics can also be associations in the form of abbreviations, or even rhymes or songs. I admit that when I need to alphabetize something, I still start to sing in my head the ABC song I learned as a kid.

Acronyms are another form of mnemonics and are abbreviations made up of the first letter of each word. When I first arrived in Singapore from the United States, I was frequently confused by all of the mnemonics people used in their everyday conversations. It felt like people were speaking a different language: "I had a CCA this morning, so I took the MRT from my HDB to SGH because there would be peak hour traffic on the PIE to the CTE and I also wanted to avoid the ERP" (see footnote if you need a translation).[2] I marveled at how creative people could be with their acronyms, almost reaching an art form in Singapore.

Mnemonics are not only associated with words but witty phrases as well. Phrases that are outrageous and even obscene enough to make you blush seem to be especially effective for memory. "Some Lovers Try Positions That They Can't Handle" represents the bones in the hand (Scaphoid, Lunate, Triquetrum, Pisiform, Trapezium, Trapezoid, Capitate, Hamate). While you can find many examples of mnemonics on the internet, coming up with your own that have additional meaning to you are even more powerful. You can also find free mnemonic generators online (go to our www.strategiclearn.org website and look under "Additional Resources"), which can help inspire you if you need some additional help.

Learning scientists have found that as we encode our bits of information into memories, other information comes along at the same time. This associated information can be connected subconsciously. The scientific

---

[2] For the non-Singaporeans, this sentence is translated: I had a co-curricular (school associated) activity this morning so I took the Mass Rapid Transit (subway) from my Housing and Development Board (public housing flat) to Singapore General Hospital because there would be peak hour traffic on the Pan-Island Expressway to the Central Expressway (Singapore highways) and I also wanted to avoid the Electronic Road Pricing (electronic toll).

term for this is "spreading activation." For many, smells are an exceptionally efficient trigger for memories. When I encounter the scent of a particular type of freshly cut, slightly wet grass, it brings me immediately back to memories of bicycle rides to my early morning classes at Stanford.

Known as the "Proust effect," it is thought that the brain's smell center, called the olfactory bulb, is closely located and connected with the amygdala and hippocampus (Chu & Downes, 2002). The amygdala and hippocampus are the areas of the brain responsible for memories and emotions.[3]

Encoding specificity

Your choice of where you study can affect memory as well. This phenomenon is known as encoding specificity. This principle states that when learning, environmental cues present at the time will enhance that memory if they are also available when it is retrieved (Tulving & Thomson, 1973). In a study of deep-sea divers learning the same information either underwater or at the side of a pool, they were able to recall the information better when tested in a similar circumstance to when they learned it. Since the divers needed the information underwater, the study concluded that the divers should learn it underwater as well (Godden and Baddeley, 1975).

Students often choose to study in the most comfortable environment they can create for themselves, for example, reading in the comfort of their bed or studying with their favorite music blasting away on their headphones. Instead, they might benefit from the principle of encoding specificity by studying in an environment similar to where they will need to recall what they are learning. Some students may even try to study in the same room where the examination will take place. This learning strategy improves recall and doesn't require much additional work on your part.

---

[3] I've not tried this one myself, but I have a colleague who uses different colognes when he studies specific topics in chemistry. He claims he associates the smells with particular topics and it helps him remember better!

Chapter 4

Figure 1. Encoding Specificity: Studying in the place where you will be asked to recall that information may give your memory a boost.

> The encoding specificity principle states that we can better retrieve information from memory through cues encoded for retrieval during memorizing. This indeed worked for me. For example, I tend to forget what I want to do when I go into a new room. However, after backtracking to my original location, I can recall what I wanted to do initially. In this case the location context was providing me with cues to trigger my memory.
>
> **Student, Year 4, NUS Faculty of Engineering**

Preparing your mind for connections

When we initially encode information in our brains, the more it can be connected with things we already know, the easier it will be to find again in our memory. It is like putting a tag on something you write on social media like Instagram or create on Evernote. You just need to remember the tag to more easily search for and find it.

The Metacognitive Cycle — Encoding Memory

Having an overall framework and context for the information you intend to learn will help you encode that information better. Students can take advantage of this principle by preparing ahead of time for their lecture or class. Most students don't realize that doing work anticipating what you intend to learn in class is a very efficient use of time. Pre-class preparation helps create more robust connections between things you already know and the new material encountered in the classroom. This preparation will help you leave class with a richer understanding of the materials presented.

I recommend that before the course begins, students should review any closely connected knowledge that is required as a course prerequisite. Review the course goals and objectives and write down everything you already know about the subject you are about to learn. It doesn't matter if you don't know very much at this time. (After all, you haven't started the class yet!) If you know how to draw a mind map (see Appendix B), this is a practical format to record this review. Many students use a mind map to summarize what they know and visually understand how it connects to other things they already know.

Some of what you write down may just be an impression or guess, and perhaps you are afraid that many parts you write down will be incorrect. But don't worry, that's fine. When you put these thoughts down on paper, you become more alert to the times when things you are learning conflict with what you thought you already knew. This can also help you correct information that you didn't initially understand very well. Just be sure to correct any incorrect understandings before the exam!

Quickly read the required or recommended chapters before rather than after the class lecture. Alternatively, watch a short YouTube video on the subject. Most students don't prioritize time in their learning plans to prepare for their class lectures. Some think this is too difficult or time-consuming and a waste of time. At the very least, I recommend glancing at the required or recommended readings in the textbook of your choice, paying attention to the chapter subheadings to understand how the author has organized the materials. Keep this organization in your mind as you attend to your classroom work.

There are a few other tips that will also help get the most from your class time. Pay close attention to the figures and tables in the required readings since they usually cover the main points. There may even be practice questions at the end of the chapter. If so, try to guess what the right answer might be! If the book is well written, these questions should highlight the most important ideas in the chapter. Alternatively, search the subject you are about to learn about on the internet and start by quickly reading a synopsis of the materials.

I know you are asking in disbelief, "Is he really telling me to study ahead of class? I can barely study after class!" This suggestion will undoubtedly feel weird to you because you have previously learned just to show up to class as if you were going to the movies. You think it is your teacher's job to fill your head with everything you need to know: "It is not my responsibility to teach myself and work hard to learn!"

However, to make this study technique helpful to you, you will need to get out of the passive mindset. This trick will give you an advantage in making the most of your time spent in class learning.

If you are someone like me who "doesn't get much from a lecture" and feels overwhelmed by the material, unable to follow the discussion or frequently confused by the professor, this technique will help you even more. And if you are taking a class taught in a language other than your primary language, this tip can make a huge difference in your learning. Once you get into this habit, you might even realize that it helps you so much that you prioritize and commit to even more time preparing ahead of the class in your learning plans.

Strategies to improve encoding

Strategize how you can best initiate your learning process and efficiently encode memories into your brain. Incorporate these ideas into your learning plan. Practice and see what works best for you, and under what circumstances. For the rote memorization techniques described earlier in this chapter, I suggest trying several different ones out and practicing what works for you. "Exercising your brain" by repeatedly using these skills will allow you to become more expert at developing the memory cues and associations that work for you.

Exercising your brain doesn't directly strengthen your overall critical thinking skills on other non-related matters. Playing lots of chess doesn't necessarily make your mathematical skills stronger. Nevertheless, the brain can change. Studies reveal that when it learns new things, the anatomical part responsible in the brain, like a muscle, can grow in size (Li, Legault & Litcofsky, 2014).

If you choose to work on your memory techniques, your ability to retrieve memorized items will improve. It improves because you have learned and practiced new systems that better encode and then retrieve items at a later time. But like everything else in this book, it will take some time for you to develop!

Consider asking your most nerdy friends to form a group/memory club to compete with each other on memorizing long lists of things (such as poems, anatomical parts, people, capitals of countries, numbers like Pi or area codes, etc.). The winner shares with the others how they did it! You'll develop a more extensive repertoire of ways you can remember things. Impress your other friends with your new memory skills![4]

Attention

There are several other important influences on our ability to effectively encode that we haven't talked about yet. In addition to encoding specificity such as the environment where we study, Ebbinghaus observed during his memory experiments that our emotional state (ability to focus, fascination, etc.) at the time we are learning influences our memory for the event.

---

[4] I think at the very least, some of these memory skills make for a good party trick for your friends, but I also acknowledge that you and your friends may have a different concept of what you consider interesting and fun.

> *"Very great is the dependence of retention and reproduction upon the intensity of the attention and interest which were attached to the mental states the first time they were present. The burnt child shuns the fire, and the dog which has been beaten runs from the whip, after a single vivid experience. People in whom we are interested we may see daily and yet not be able to recall the colour of their hair or of their eyes…Our information comes almost exclusively from the observation of extreme and especially striking cases."*
> — Ebbinghaus —

Ebbinghaus' astute observations about the influence that your mental state, focus and attention have on encoding and learning will be covered in more depth later in this book (Chapter 8: Health and Well-Being).

Edu-tainment

Memories of extremely entertaining content such as a great book, a suspenseful movie, a hilarious comic or even an exceptional lecture grab our attention and are easier to remember and recall. When these experiences are novel and dramatic enough, we described them as "unforgettable." Unfortunately, these truly remarkable experiences are uncommon. Only a limited number of things that we encounter over our lifetime can stand out enough and be genuinely novel enough to be remembered for a long time. The reason the entertainment business is so challenging is that our minds quickly find similar materials (no matter how well presented) to be "boring and forgettable." We highly value (i.e., usually pay them lots of attention and money) entertainers for their ability to stand out from others, and easily recall their work.

We have real limits on the amount of information that we remember using this novel entertainment path. Most educators do not possess the skills necessary to deliver their instructional materials well enough to be remembered in this way. As a result, students need to depend on methods other than entertainment to encode information from a typical faculty lecture.

Once we have encoded bits of information in our memory, are there other things we can do to further improve recall when we need it later on? The next couple of chapters cover how to do precisely that.

Summary: Chapter 4

Our brain encodes the information that we learn in mysterious ways that are not always obvious to our conscious mind. The subconscious connections we make while learning can also be consciously utilized to improve our recall (using strategies such as chunking, mnemonics, and encoding specificity). Attention is another important aspect of encoding our memories and will be discussed further in Chapter 8.

References

Chu, S., & Downes, J. J. (2002). Proust nose best: Odors are better cues of autobiographical memory. *Memory & Cognition*, **30**(4), 511–518.

Foer, J. (2012). *Moonwalking with Einstein: The Art and Science of Remembering Everything*. Penguin: New York.

Godden, D. R., & Baddeley, A. D. (1975). Context-dependent memory in two natural environments: On land and underwater. *British Journal of Psychology*, **66**(3), 325–331.

Li, P., Legault, J., & Litcofsky, K. A. (2014). Neuroplasticity as a function of second language learning: Anatomical changes in the human brain. *Cortex*, **58**, 301–324.

Tulving, E., & Thomson, D. M. (1973). Encoding specificity and retrieval processes in episodic memory. *Psychological Review*, **80**(5), 352.

Chapter 5

The Metacognitive Cycle — Flattening Out the Forgetting Curve

Myth: Learning should be as easy as possible for the learner to learn. Great teachers make learning easy for me.
Reality: Great teachers make learning just hard enough.

The myth that learning should be as easy as possible is one of the toughest to convince learners that it is a myth. And it is one of the most critical learning myths to bust. On one level, this idea makes a lot of sense and, therefore, is exceedingly believable. It is a belief that is widely and firmly held by most students and teachers. However, though it seems correct, research consistently finds this statement to be wrong.

As we know all too well, after our brain encodes and stores a memory, we immediately and unceasingly start to forget it. We learned in the last chapter that the connections we make with any new information can influence how easy or difficult it will be to recall that memory in the future. As Ebbinghaus documented, after we initially encode information, there are things we can immediately do to influence the shape of our forgetting curve. It is possible to flatten the curve and make our memories more durable and longer lasting. Active learning, when we engage in some way with the information rather

Chapter 5

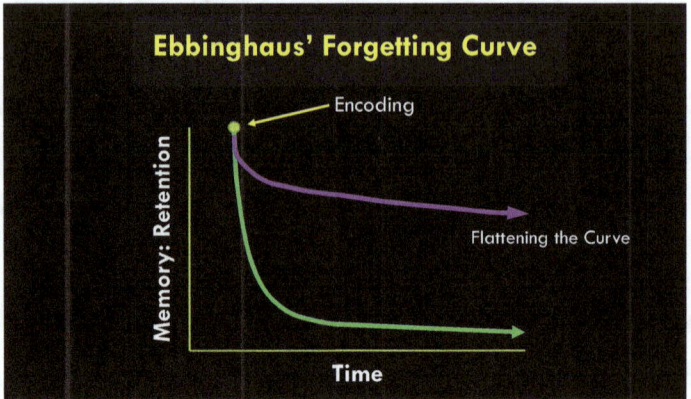

Figure 1. There are several techniques that can "flatten" the forgetting curve, and make memories last longer. These include techniques covered in the previous chapter that occur before or at the time of encoding memory. The strategies described in this chapter occur shortly after encoding and also serve to make those memories more durable.

than just passively take it in, is the key method to optimizing learning for this aspect of the forgetting curve.

Forgetting is not all bad!

Before we go any further into how we can alter the forgetting curve, I should clarify that forgetting isn't all bad. In fact, it is a good thing that we forget things. You might think that those rare individuals who struggle to forget things (a medical condition called hyperthymesia) will do brilliantly in school. In reality, they have a hard time learning new things. They seem to remember every mundane fact and find themselves stuck in a world of their past. Their ability to consciously remember some new things, such as information needed for a school examination, might even be below average.

Their brains don't seem to have the mechanism to let less important matters fade away and allow only the most essential information to remain. It is easy to understand how, as a result, they have more work to do to sort out the useful from the useless information also stored there. Our brains are programmed so that we will eventually forget the information that we don't often use! It is an elegant solution to our limitation of having a finite amount of memory.

The Metacognitive Cycle — Flattening Out the Forgetting Curve

Homo sapiens were able to become the dominant species on the planet because of the human brain and our ability to think. Other creatures on the earth are faster runners and swimmers; many are stronger, taller or more agile. It is our brain that has evolved to develop the social systems that allow us to live in the most varied environments on earth, utilize natural resources and harness other animals for our benefit. The cost of this brainpower is substantial energy demands by the brain, but the benefits of committing resources to fueling our thoughts are obvious from an evolutionary perspective.

Conserving energy

In recognition of the considerable energy requirements it has, the brain reflectively tries to conserve energy when possible. The body attempts to prioritize that energy for its most valuable intellectual or physical tasks. In other words, our brain is naturally wired to be lazy when it can! As we will learn in Chapter 7 on self-regulation, those who can strategically overcome this natural "laziness" of the brain and study when they would rather be in bed resting or hanging out with friends can achieve academic success beyond those who are their intellectual equals or better.

Our lazy brain does not always realize when it needs to further process bits of information so it can retrieve them later. It tries to convince us that it has done enough to remember that information for the future. And as we demonstrated in the Day at the Zoo activity, our brain can't easily distinguish what it can only recognize from what it can recall. As a result, our mind easily deceives us, fooling us to think that our memory of an item is secure and no further work is necessary. We are then stunned and disappointed in the future when we can't remember something when we want to!

If our brain naturally forgets what we don't use, it must do additional work to keep the memories we want to keep from rapidly decaying! The lazy brain wants to encode the material quickly, and not think about it again. It urges you to save encoding time by multi-tasking (does sitting in the back of a lecture hall trying to listen to your professor while simultaneously scrolling through the latest social media platform sound familiar?). The truth: The more effort you put into actively processing the material, rather than just passively staring at it for just a moment, the more durable you will make that memory.

Making additional connections

In the last chapter, we covered some techniques such as encoding specificity, chunking and mnemonics that learners can use to prepare the brain before or at the time of the encoding process. Some of the techniques I described in the last chapter can be used after the initial encoding as well. I'm currently learning how to play the guitar and have tried to memorize the notes of the strings: E A D G B E. After I initially encoded the notes, I realized I still couldn't recall them, so I decided I'd better use the mnemonic I found on the internet: "**Eat All Day Get Big Easy**." If only the rest of learning to play the guitar could be helped by mnemonics! Now, we will cover some other ways the brain can make those encoded memories longer lasting.

One of the main techniques used by memory champions is called "memory palace." In addition to the various connections learned at the same time as the initial encoding of the material, these elite memorizers subsequently create new connections with things they already know well. It is these added connections that enhance their ability to recall the memory later. The term "palace" refers to a physical space already well known to the individual (such as their home or workplace), and easy for them to imagine themselves walking through it. As they walk through their palace, they mentally place objects that remind them of what they want to remember. They later retrieve these items in the same order as they imagine walking through their space. The extra work after the initial encoding of information spent visualizing objects in a familiar setting makes your memory for those items exceptionally durable.

If you use this technique, I think you will be surprised how much you find you remember things that you would otherwise have quickly forgotten!

Depth of Processing Activity
(Approximate Duration: 5–7 minutes over 20 minutes time)

URL: www.strategiclearn.org
(go to Activities/Depth of Processing)

Aim: Demonstration of the effect that depth of processing has on memory and learning.

Instructions: You will need a piece of paper and pen for this activity. Watch the video on this activity and then complete the task using the instructions given on the website. Please report your score, we will compare groups using different methods to learn.

Depth of processing

Learners participating in this activity above were divided into two groups. One group was instructed to process the word more deeply than the other. They had to think about the meaning of the word and imagine the emotions that it conjured up. They then needed to decide if those emotions were pleasant or unpleasant. The other group just needed to visually recognize whether the first letter of the word was in the capital or lowercase form. It wasn't necessary to read the word, or understand what it meant. From this real world experiment, you can see that the learners who more deeply processed the words remembered those words better.

The psychology literature calls this phenomenon "depth of processing." The more or "deeper" that the brain works on something, the more it actively engages with the material, the more durable that memory becomes.

This additional processing of the content is not what the brain likes to do. Still, strategic learners have figured out that if they process the information further after initially encoding, it makes what they have learned more durable. These individuals are not fooled by their lazy brain into thinking that they have learned it well enough by passively encoding it. They recognize that they must employ deeper processing when it is important to remember something. There are many ways that one can further process what is learned to make your memory for that item more durable.

Depth of processing is another way to describe the differences between active and passive learning. The term active learning refers to the instructional methods (pedagogy) that require the learner to further process the information learned and think about it in different ways. Active learning encompasses many different possible activities: for example, answering a question or two posed by the teacher (or, even better, raised by yourself!), or working on a team project that uses the learned materials to answer a problem or create something new. Passive learning, sometimes known as "traditional" education, is when instructors simply rely on "teaching by telling." Although it is the teaching method (pedagogy) we all grew up with, there has been considerable research over the past several decades which all demonstrates the same thing: Active learning makes the memory for that material more durable than passive learning.

Don't simply read and re-read

One of the most common study-technique time-wasters used by students is to simply read and then later re-read those same book chapters. Sometimes, students accompany this read/re-read technique with highlighting, to make it easier for them to note which sections they have already read. They believe that by highlighting the most important text they can later focus their eyes just on the highlighted text. They will then be able to get through their study of the material quicker (and more efficiently) when it is time to review it.

Unfortunately, many won't do the additional processing to determine the most critical text and instead will highlight so much of the book that the entire page is a solid yellow! It is easy to highlight everything when your eyes read the material thoughtlessly. But without any further depth of processing of the content, all you are doing with extensive highlighting is verifying that you have seen it before, not that you understand or can recall it.

The Metacognitive Cycle — Flattening Out the Forgetting Curve

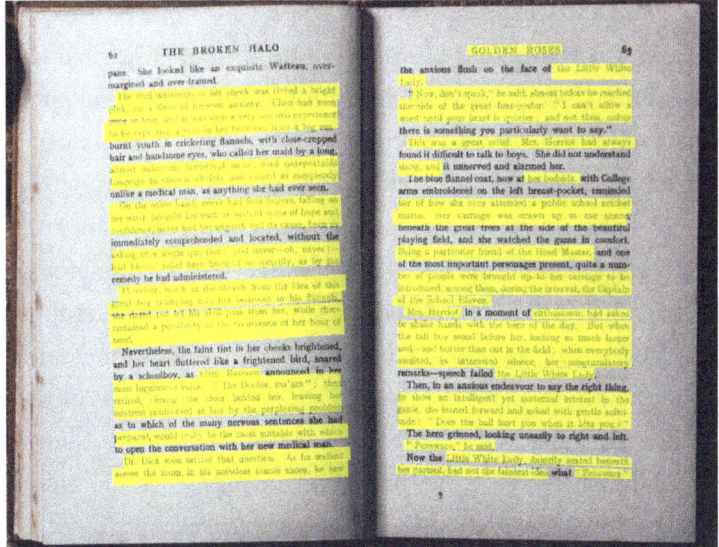

Figure 2. Looks familiar?

When we review the highlighted text without doing any further processing (such as asking additional questions about it or answering questions about this material), we aren't significantly improving our ability to recall this information at a later time. When students study by re-reading the highlighted text, it feels highly efficient. And as you recognize the words, it all feels familiar, deceiving you into thinking you have learned it well. Unfortunately, as in our Day at the Zoo activity, recognizing that you have seen the text is easy, but it doesn't mean that you can recall it in an exam.

Interleaving

What is very interesting to me, and one of the reasons that inspired me to write this book, is that our perceptions of learning are often wrong. Scientific research has repeatedly documented that we have a hard time recognizing when we are learning well.

There is a story about a successful baseball coach whose teams won many championships. His secret? He made his batters practice in a way that they didn't like. Before this coach, the traditional method for baseball batters to practice hitting a baseball was to have a coach throw one type of pitch (for example, a fastball) over and over again until the batter learned to hit the ball successfully. The coach would then throw a different type of pitch (say, a curveball) until the batter was successfully hitting that type of pitch as well. And then on to a different kind of pitch and so on. In this traditional (blocked) practice, the batters more easily learned to hit the baseball. They felt a real sense of accomplishment and could see how they learned to hit the ball.

However, the successful coach did something very different in practice. Instead of giving a series of one type of pitch at a time before switching to another, he made the batters do something more challenging. He mixed up the pitches. The result? The batters hated it and complained bitterly. They were not as able to hit the ball as well as they previously did in practice. They missed that sense of accomplishment and previous success of blocked practice. At first, they tried to blame their coach for their worse performance. But what happened in their practice was different from what happened in the real game. These batters learned that in the actual game setting, they were able to hit much better than before, and they won more games (Hall, Domingues & Cavazos, 1994).

This learning technique is known as "interleaving," and it applies not only to baseball and other sports but to learning in general. When topics are easily confused with each other (is the next pitch a fastball or a curveball?), mixing them up makes it more challenging to learn. The learner has to work harder to be successful. However, when it is time to retrieve their learning later, whether it is during a game or an examination, it is easier. Interleaving similar topics such as applying the right mathematical functions or recognizing the difference between similar concepts like RNA vs DNA replication will result in better learning and a more durable memory (Rohrer, 2012).[1]

---

[1] A practical note: Incorporating interleaving into your learning plans is very tricky and difficult to get right. First, interleaving refers to mixing subjects/topics that are easily confused (such as different baseball pitches), rather than two or more completely separate topics or disciplines. Interleaving these topics makes you think harder in order to differentiate between them, for example, having to select the correct mathematical equation to use to solve a problem. Interleaving also suffers from the "Goldilocks problem" of needing to get it "just right." A certain level of proficiency with the material is first required. You can imagine if someone has never played baseball before, and the coach is throwing all sorts of different pitches to hit, that the practice could be too hard, and you would get frustrated and not learn anything. When you use interleaving, it is important for it not to be too little or too much, but as Goldilocks would say, "just right."

The Metacognitive Cycle — Flattening Out the Forgetting Curve

> "When learning science subjects, one concept might sound familiar to another that had been mentioned in an earlier lecture. It is important that when we do our self-study, we start differentiating these concepts so as to not be confused during the exam. For example, in Statistics, we need to apply the correct distribution function formula depending on whether the random variable is discrete or non-discrete. Instead of writing the formulas and dividing them based on the chapter chronology in my notebook, I grouped them according to similarity and used interleaving to start differentiating them within these groups."

Student, Year 2, NUS Faculty of Science, Mathematics

Desirable difficulties

Professor Robert Bjork coined the term "desirable difficulties" to explain this general concept about learning. (Bjork & Bjork, 2011) The teacher's task is to teach the material at a level difficult enough to challenge (desirable) but not overwhelm. Interleaving is an example of how the learner learns more if they struggle with the material just enough and can process it at a deeper level.

Another interesting related example of this principle is the concept of "learning styles" — the idea of improving education by personalizing instruction to fit individual learning differences. Learning styles are the ways in which we seem to most easily take in information and encode into memory. There are many different models of learning styles; one of the most well-known depends on which sensory modality we feel we learn best using. This model assigns learners in the following groups: Visual (by graphs, pictures, symbols); Auditory (by lectures, discussions); Tactile (by experiment, doing, touching).

Teaching to one's preferred learning style has been repeatedly studied over the past several decades. Although it seems to make sense that is should, there is no evidence that educating students using their preferred learning styles is effective (Cuevas, 2015).[2] Again, we intuitively believe that making things easy for us to

---

[2] Despite the widespread belief in the idea that teaching should fit students' preferred learning styles, and the subsequent and considerable investments in this concept by schools

learn is effective, but evidence shows that learning is best when it is made just hard enough.

We are clueless about optimal learning

A fascinating feature of desirable difficulties is that when learning is optimized in this way, learners generally don't recognize the learning gains. In fact, like those baseball batters, many feel the opposite — that their education is impaired by it (Simon & Bjork, 2001)! In one experiment, subjects learned to recognize different artists using blocked versus interleaved practice. As you would now expect, 85% of participants who learned to characterize different artists' styles using interleaving did the same or better than those taught using blocked practice to identify the artist responsible for a painting they had not seen before. When the researchers asked the subjects which learning practice was more effective however, 83% were convinced that they had learned better using blocked practice (Kornell & Bjork, 2008).

Studies looking at other teaching strategies have reported similar findings. Recently, undergraduate students at Harvard participated in two different experimental teaching designs: one that featured active learning and another that used a more traditional, passive lecture. Again, while students performed better on exams using the active learning classroom (as would be predicted from the scientific literature), they nevertheless were convinced that they had learned better in the passive classroom format (Deslauriers *et al.*, 2019). Despite multiple reports over the past several decades documenting the limitations of students judging what constitutes optimal learning, it seems like we are shocked each time a new study makes this finding. As I said, this myth is tough to bust!

---

throughout the world, there have been numerous research studies and repeated reviews published in the literature which fail to demonstrate any improvements in learning. The concept continues to maintain a hold on educators and students because it feels like it is correct. For example, I "feel" I am a better visual than auditory learner. I remember less from listening to a lecture and remember more easily from reading a book. Therefore, it makes sense that I would do better by primarily learning using my most natural sensory modality. However, at best, studies show that any positive effect of learning based on one's favorite learning style is small. Therefore, any effort toward improving learning is best devoted to other practices that have a larger effect.

Shallow versus deeper levels of processing

Bloom's Taxonomy is a set of models covering three different learning domains, first devised by a committee of educators in the 1950s. The most notable of these models covered the cognitive domain. The cognitive domain was subsequently revised in 2001 and classified learning into the following levels (Krathwohl & Anderson, 2009):

Bloom's Taxonomy

CREATE: re-assembling different elements of facts/thoughts to form a new idea(s)
EVALUATION: judging ideas based on criteria such as validity, outcomes, evidence
ANALYSIS: breaking down information into fundamental components, sometimes known as "first principle thinking"
APPLY: using facts to solve a new problem, connect with other facts
UNDERSTAND: defining, organizing, describing facts, teaching others
REMEMBER: memorizing facts, without necessarily understanding what they mean

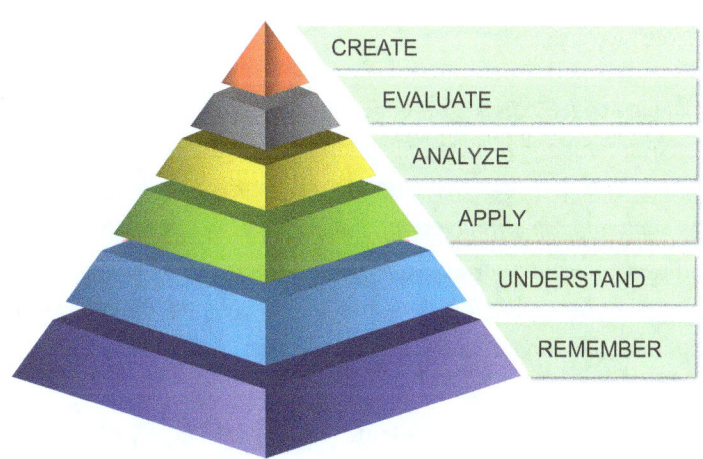

Figure 3. Bloom's Taxonomy based on the Krathwohl and Anderson revisions.

Chapter 5

Knowledge is considered the foundational base of the cognitive domain, with deeper levels of skills required as you move toward the top of the pyramid. There is a debate in the literature about whether or not these levels genuinely represent discrete hierarchical levels or not (I believe it is an overstatement to think the lowest levels of the hierarchy aren't as important as the higher levels). Nevertheless, what makes Bloom's Taxonomy still widely quoted by educators is that they nicely describe different types of thinking.

On occasion, I hear students say, "Just tell me what I need to learn, and I'll memorize it for the exam!" They are confused by the difference between memory and learning and believe that being told by their teacher what to memorize is a practical shortcut to learning. What they don't realize is that this method does not result in deeper and more durable learning. They may be able to successfully memorize things for the upcoming examination. However, without understanding the material at a deeper level, without actively processing the information in some way, the memory of this information will more quickly fade away.

All upper levels of Bloom's Taxonomy represent processes that can deepen your level of learning. The "Remember" level is the focus of traditional education and often represents too much of what is taught in schools. Memorization becomes learning when study incorporates these other higher-level processes. Information acquired using these different levels of Bloom's Taxonomy are not as easily forgotten and will advance your thinking and learning skills.

> *Thinking about Bloom's taxonomy, I realized I usually stayed at the first step (Remembering). Instead I should incorporate understanding by creating links between the content I was learning. After memorizing and understanding the content, I also pretended to be the teacher and walked around my house teaching myself out aloud, as if I was doing a presentation. Teaching myself really helped me improve my understanding and memory for the content. I was really impressed.*
>
> **Student, Year 4, NUS Faculty of Arts and Social Sciences, Psychology**

The Metacognitive Cycle — Flattening Out the Forgetting Curve

The more you know, the more you can learn

The best students have learned that working hard to learn at a deeper level is a good strategy, even though it is natural to believe in the opposite — that optimal learning should be as easy as possible. I think it would be "fairer" if those who had more to learn had an easier time catching up with everyone else's knowledge. However, it doesn't work that way! The twist here is that the harder you work to go to a deeper level, the easier subsequent learning becomes. Great students get their academic head start from their natural intelligence and hard work, but as they carry on, what they realize is: "The more you know, the more you can learn." They keep becoming better and better students as they learn more.

Making deeper connections with what you already know allows you to retrieve added knowledge at a later time more easily. The smarter students have a natural advantage over others because they have more previous knowledge to connect new information with. For this reason, the smartest kids in a class continue to have the advantage in getting the best grades.

As we have discussed, active learning is hard work, and our natural tendency is to conserve our energy when possible so that it is available for other tasks. Unless you are already the smartest kid in your class, to learn better than everyone else will take considerable effort on your part. You will need to commit yourself to go deep with your learning materials and no longer be satisfied that you have read it once or twice and think you know and can recall it. You should try to prepare ahead of each class as much as you can, not just after it is over. You'll get more out of the classroom time with your teacher.

In the next chapter, we will finish covering our different learning strategies. We have been saving the best for last: the strategies that "reset" the Forgetting Curve. This is one of the most efficient techniques you can do to remember (and learn) better.

Summary: Chapter 5

To optimize our learning, the material learned must neither be too easy nor too hard to learn, but just right. The more effort we take to process the information we learn (by asking questions about it, using it to solve problems, mixing it up with other similar information/interleaving), the more durable in our memory it becomes. This is known as increasing the depth of processing. The positive effect of this strategy on memory is often unrecognized by the learner.

References

Bjork, E. L., & Bjork, R. A. (2011). Making things hard on yourself, but in a good way: Creating desirable difficulties to enhance learning. In *Psychology and the Real World: Essays Illustrating Fundamental Contributions to Society,* M. A. Gernsbacher, R. W. Pew, L. M. Hough, J. R. Pomerantz (eds.), 59–68, Worth Publishers: New York.

Cuevas, J. (2015). Is learning styles-based instruction effective? A comprehensive analysis of recent research on learning styles. *Theory and Research in Education,* **13**(3), 308–333.

Deslauriers, L., McCarty, L. S., Miller, K., Callaghan, K., & Kestin, G. (2019). Measuring actual learning versus feeling of learning in response to being actively engaged in the classroom. *Proceedings of the National Academy of Sciences,* **116**(39), 19251–19257.

Hall, K. G., Domingues, D. A., & Cavazos, R. (1994). Contextual interference effects with skilled baseball players. *Perceptual and Motor Skills,* **78**(3), 835–841.

Krathwohl, D. R., & Anderson, L. W. (2009). *A Taxonomy for Learning, Teaching, and Assessing: A Revision of Bloom's Taxonomy of Educational Objectives.* Longman: New York.

Kornell, N., & Bjork, R. A. (2008). Learning concepts and categories: Is spacing the "enemy of induction"? *Psychological Science,* **19**(6), 585–592.

Rohrer, D. (2012). Interleaving helps students distinguish among similar concepts. *Educational Psychology Review,* **24**(3), 355–367.

Simon, D. A., & Bjork, R. A. (2001). Metacognition in motor learning. *Journal of Experimental Psychology: Learning, Memory, and Cognition,* **27**(4), 907.

Chapter 6

The Metacognitive Cycle — Resetting the Forgetting Curve

Myth: Cramming works for me, so I'm going to have fun and just study right before the test.

Reality: Cramming does work, but there is a caveat you should understand.

One of the most significant findings from Ebbinghaus' forgetting studies is that your memory can be "reset" back to a higher level by merely reviewing the same information at a later time. Therefore, a quick reminder can efficiently boost the memory after it has faded. The learning strategies discussed in this chapter should be an important part of everyone's learning plans.

The phenomenon known as "spaced learning" is when things are learned over multiple, separate sessions distributed over time, rather than "blocked learning," which is to study everything at one time (Cepeda et al., 2006; Maddox, 2016). The most common blocked learning method students use is to "cram" right before the examination.

Chapter 6

The boost that comes from spacing capitalizes on the method that the brain uses to filter out what is valuable to remember from what isn't: The brain more easily retains memories that come up time and time again. And presumably, those facts that come up time and time again are things you want your mind to remember better!

Cramming works! (Sort of)

Students can be fooled into not spacing their learning because their experience with cramming is that it works! What makes cramming so attractive to some students is that they can goof off until the very last moment, stay up all night to prepare for the upcoming examination and still do well enough the next day. Their last-minute cram sessions will indeed provide that memory encoding that might get them successfully through the exam the following morning before they forget everything.

I understand when students tell me that they would rather just have fun, keep procrastinating with their study plans and only get serious right before the examination. Why try so hard to self-discipline and follow a

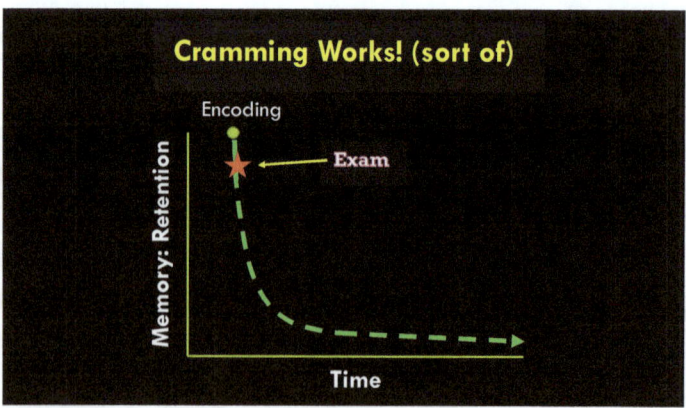

Figure 1. Cramming works! If the exam is taken before you naturally forget what you have learned.

The Metacognitive Cycle — Resetting the Forgetting Curve

well-intended plan to spread out your study over the entire course? Instead, why not just stay up all night and try to memorize as much as possible for the test. Then, the next morning, hope that the test covers what you studied the previous night, and then "brain dump" all you can remember on to the exam. When these students get their grades back, some have done well enough this way.

If cramming works, why don't I recommend it for everyone? What learners don't realize is that when they try to pack in all their learning at the last minute, they might remember it for the examination immediately after their cram session, however, they will forget that material more easily and more quickly after the exam. Tests typically only include information recently covered in class, so they won't have much awareness about how fast they forgot. Unless their next exam again covers the material that they have just crammed into their heads, they won't have any idea about what and how much they have forgotten.

For information that you don't care about and are convinced that you will never use again, you might think it is okay to block your learning and

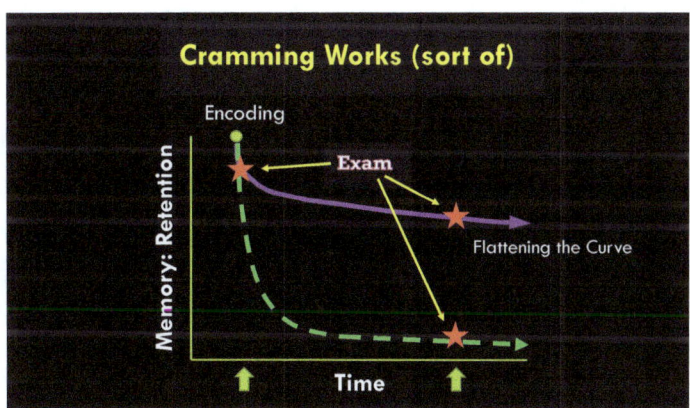

Figure 2. Flattening the Curve: After cramming, if you test immediately you might do well (Green line). But if you test later, there will be a difference to how much you remember as compared to if you used strategies that flatten or reset the curve (Purple line).

cram for the test, pass the course, then forget what you learned and get on with your life. Unfortunately, most of us don't have great insight into what information we'll need for our future. My suggestion? Especially for information that you would like to remember for a more extended time, it is best to space out your timing when you review the material. It doesn't take any more study time from your overall schedule to space your learning over time; it just requires planning and discipline. We will discuss in the rest of this chapter how your memory of information will last longer if you space your learning.

Not everything is equally important to re-learn

A useful strategy along with resetting your forgetting curve is to come to a decision about what information is important to return to and what is not.

The Italian economist Vilfredo Pareto noticed many instances where 80% of results stem from 20% of possible conditions. He based that idea on his initial observation that 20% of the people owned approximately 80% of the land in his country. This observation, now named after him, led him to find other examples of this association.

The field of quality control/optimization adopted the Pareto Principle after noticing most poor-quality outcomes result from a small but central set of issues. They realized that identifying and prioritizing fixing those issues first would be the most efficient way to improve quality. Although sometimes known as the 80/20 rule, the Pareto Principle does not always follow this exact percentage. Nevertheless, the important takeaway from the Pareto Principle as applied to learning is that not everything taught is equally important. You can be more efficient with your learning if you can determine what areas to focus on and which areas to spend less time on.

Great learners continuously evaluate the material they are studying to determine how important it is. As I have mentioned, when the brain repeatedly encounters the same information, it automatically registers it as more important. Something said by the teacher in class and found again in the reading is reinforced in the brain's memory.

The Metacognitive Cycle — Resetting the Forgetting Curve

Instructors usually tailor their examinations to cover the most important topics. Strategic learners find ways to figure out "how to think like my instructor" and determine the most critical material to concentrate their time on. However, most instructors will get irritated when students attempt to ascertain what to study by simply asking them: "Is this going to be on the test?" So, don't do that.

Instead, strategic learners note the examples that the teacher discussed in class and they look through the required textbooks and look at the topics most of the writing is devoted to. Book authors emphasize specific topics by including tables and figures about them, so these are also valuable areas to review. A well-written article or book chapter will in some way signal the most important information to the reader.

The best learners consciously sort out and prioritize the information they should learn well. When students go to class and listen to the instructor, they are looking for subtle clues to determine what is important: for example, when the instructor says, "Pay attention; this information will be on the exam!" But other clues may not be so obvious, such as the amount of time spent discussing a particular topic in class. This can indicate where to concentrate your study.

Finally (and to the great horror of many of my shy students in Singapore), I suggest that you meet your instructor during office hours and ask questions in person. In this setting, your instructor will be more likely to clue you in to areas to commit your study time on. If the instructor is one on one with you, they are more likely to tell you when a topic you are asking them questions about is not so important. While this is NOT a normal part of the culture of learning in Singapore, I think this is an enormous missed opportunity for students. I tell my students that if you graduate from your university without knowing several professors well, you have not made the most of your education.[1]

---

[1] When I do have the opportunity to meet with students, we usually start with questions that have come up in class. After those initial questions, the topic of conversation can be wide-ranging, and I always enjoy it very much. I know most of my faculty colleagues are also flattered when students stop by to talk.

Chapter 6

Implementing spaced learning

From Ebbinghaus' curve, you can understand how efficient techniques that reset memory can be (figure 3). A spaced review of the material that has already faded will not only reset the forgetting curve and make it easier to recall, it also flattens it out and makes that memory more durable and longer lasting. A double effect!

What is the optimal timing for spaced learning? Even if you could repeatedly study everything you learn every few hours until you take the examination, it would be a waste of time. You would be over-preparing, and better off doing something else with your time. Alternatively, as we discussed, spacing things too far apart so nothing is done until right before the test (cramming) does not capture the full benefits of the learning effect from spacing. The best spacing interval or "sweet spot" at which to return to the material is when it has faded but is not completely gone from the memory. In practice, this type of fine-tuning of your study is very complex to determine.

Scientists have been working on optimizing the answer to this timing problem for the past several decades. Computer technology has provided some solutions to personalized timing of spaced study. Computer programs can now use factors such as how difficult the information was initially to

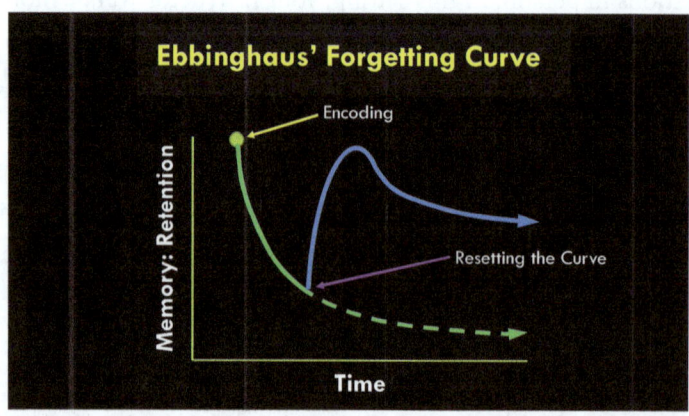

Figure 3. Resetting the Curve is very efficient learning. I highly recommend this strategy!

learn and how quickly it fades from your memory to determine when that item should be studied again. Many computerized flashcard programs and language learning apps, etc. use these types of algorithms to optimize learning by personalizing spacing to your learning (and forgetting).

For those of you who don't have or choose not to use a computerized spacing program to guide your learning, you can do well enough by approximating the spacing schedule yourself. There is no perfect schedule that works for everyone and every subject, so you will need to adapt this for your circumstances and experience. It is probably more important to space your learning than to figure out the exact length of time to space (Karpicke & Bauernschmidt, 2011). My general, practical recommendation for a typical undergraduate course would be to briefly review what you learned on the day following the lecture. Then determine the time between when you first learned the material and when you want to maximally recall it again (usually for the final examination date in a few months' time). Divide that time period into half or thirds, with the last review session scheduled the night before the test. And if it is something you want to remember for much longer, set a reminder to review the material somewhere between six months to a year after taking the final exam.

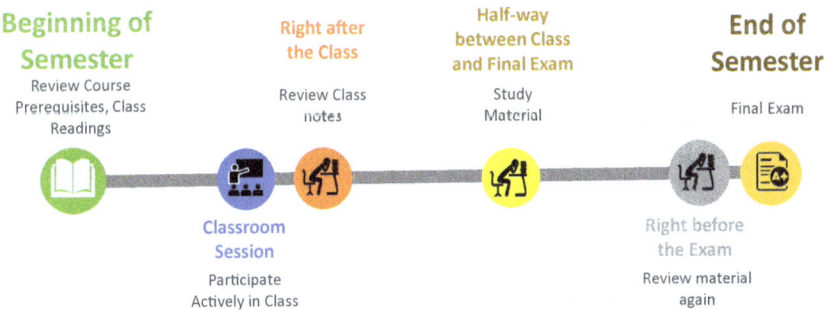

Figure 4. If you can space out your learning, you'll learn more efficiently using the same amount of study time compared to blocked learning.

Chapter 6

> In the past, I wanted to finish studying or revising content in blocks. However, I now leave breaks in-between my assignments or revision, as spacing has proven to work for me. I've now had first-hand experience with it: leaving a difficult part of my tutorial to be completed another time gave me ideas on how to tackle those problems when I saw it again.

Student, Year 3, NUS Faculty of Engineering, Architecture

The learning activities to do during spaced learning

As we have previously learned, to keep our memories from rapidly decaying, the brain must do the additional work! Simply spacing or re-exposing yourself to previously learned material by passively re-reading or re-listening to a tape of the lecture will not achieve optimal learning and resetting of the curve. You will most likely quickly forget that information once again, and therefore, it is not an efficient use of your time!

The activities you should do to reset this information in your memory after it has faded will sound familiar from the last two chapters.

My recommendations on how to best reset your memory include the same techniques used when encoding memory and making memory more durable. The activities that deepen your processing include:

- Solving problems (or homework) using what you have learned;
- Making connections between what you already know and what you are learning;
- Summarizing the material in your own words or mind map; and
- Evaluating and prioritizing the importance of different aspects of the content.

Retrieval practice

In addition to the activities stated above, perhaps the most powerful strategy you can adopt while spacing your learning is "retrieval practice." By this, you

The Metacognitive Cycle — Resetting the Forgetting Curve

literally and repeatedly practice retrieving information kept in your brain by answering practice questions. This is especially helpful if those questions are in a similar format as the ones asked during your examinations. You should commit to practicing coming up with the right answer without any prompts or clues.

We previously demonstrated the need for this practice in the Day at the Zoo activity: We are not good at distinguishing what we can just recognize from what we can recall. Our energy-preserving brain tricks us into believing we can recall every fact we recognize. In reality, the only way to know what you can recall is to try to retrieve it! And the added bonus of this learning activity is that when you practice retrieving it, you are also "resetting" your memory and making it easier to recall it at a later time. Very efficient!

From a practical standpoint, it is easy to find practice questions to assist with your retrieval practice. Textbooks often include practice questions at the end of each chapter. There are also books specifically written to provide practice questions with answers. An internet search can find reputable websites with practice questions and answers. However, the quality of these practice questions varies. Some faculty give students old tests for practice.

The deepest practice comes from creating the questions yourself and answering them. In my classes at NUS, students rarely ask any questions in class. What they don't realize is that asking questions is one of the best ways to learn the material in a way that sticks. Taking the mental energy to come up with a question and then to determine if it is a good one or not before asking compels the brain to process deeply. Asking questions is a great way to understand and remember the material better! If I could change one thing in the education systems throughout Asia, it would be to encourage more thoughtful and creative questioning in the classroom.

Given the current student culture in Singapore and the rest of Asia, I suggest taking a "baby-step." Practice asking questions in your head, and write them down as you take notes, even if you don't ask them out loud. Even better, use study teams to freely exchange questions, practice retrieving the answers from your memory and discuss the answers you come up with. That way, you'll get to practice answering more problems than if you only come up with questions yourself. If issues remain after debating answers within your study group, then you can feel confident it will be an excellent question to clarify with the faculty member in class or office hours.

Purposeful practice

It should probably go without saying that "just practicing" is not enough. The practice needs to be what is known as "purposeful practice." Practice should be purposeful, with a goal in mind, not just mindless repetition.[2] If you practice with poorly written questions or questions with the wrong answers, you will still do poorly no matter how hard you work. If you look up the answers before you try to answer them yourself, you will minimize the benefits of retrieval practice.

We tend to practice things we are already good at. It gives us a sense of accomplishment. Paradoxically, we might even spend more time on the subjects we are good at and avoid those that are harder for us. We want to be like that baseball player who likes to practice hitting a baseball using blocked practice versus the much harder interleaved practice. It feeds our sense of accomplishment and mastery. However, retrieval practice is best when focused on things we feel is important but don't already know well.

The Metacognitive Cycle: Plan

Congratulations! You now know how to set proper goals and have an approach using different strategies that can achieve those learning goals. Some of these study strategies prepare you to learn, priming your mind to better encode the information when you first encounter it. Other strategies like chunking can be used as you are learning the information for the

---

[2] Gaining expertise in an area is not just about putting in the hours of work, but also requires effective and deliberate practice. Getting immediate and helpful feedback is a key element of deliberate practice. There is a popular notion that expertise comes after 10,000 or more hours of training (Gladwell, 2008). While having a certain number of hours needed to achieve expertise is an over-simplification of research done in this area, it does reinforce the idea that with hard work and expert teaching/coaching, one can make great improvements in their knowledge and skills (Ericsson & Harwell, 2019).

first time, giving you an effective method to retrieve that information at a later time. In addition, there are things to do after your initial memory of that information has faded, such as retrieval practice. The strategies that reset your memory are especially efficient for learning and highly recommended.

Unfortunately, there are many factors that can disrupt how well your learning strategies work. So, before we complete our discussion of the rest of the Metacognitive Learning Cycle (Implement and Evaluate), we will turn to building the solid foundations that your learning strategies depend on. Let's begin with how to get ourselves ready to study in the first place: Self-Regulation.

Summary: Chapter 6

Resetting the forgetting curve by breaking up your study (spaced learning) is very efficient for learning. Prioritizing the information to be re-learned and using methods for deeper processing (such as retrieval practice rather than re-reading) while spacing your learning is recommended.

Both proper goal setting and selecting different learning strategies to implement, constitute the "Plan;" the first step of the Metacognitive Cycle.

References

Cepeda, N. J., Pashler, H., Vul, E., Wixted, J. T., & Rohrer, D. (2006). Distributed practice in verbal recall tasks: A review and quantitative synthesis. *Psychological Bulletin*, **132**(3), 354.

Ericsson, K. A., & Harwell, K. W. (2019). Deliberate practice and proposed limits on the effects of practice on the acquisition of expert performance: Why the original definition matters and recommendations for future research. *Frontiers in Psychology*, **10**(2396), doi:10.3389/fpsyg.2019.02396.

Gladwell, M. (2008). *Outliers: The Story of Success*. Little, Brown: New York.

Karpicke, J. D., & Bauernschmidt, A. (2011). Spaced retrieval: Absolute spacing enhances learning regardless of relative spacing. *Journal of Experimental Psychology: Learning, Memory, and Cognition, 37*(5), 1250.

Maddox, G. B. (2016). Understanding the underlying mechanism of the spacing effect in verbal learning: A case for encoding variability and study-phase retrieval. *Journal of Cognitive Psychology,* **28**(6), 684–706.

Chapter 7

The Foundation — Self-Regulation

Myth: My natural intelligence determines my success in life.

Reality: Intelligence is only one factor; there are others that are as or more important.

It is true that some people just don't have to work as hard as others when it comes to learning. They are naturally "smart" — they see things that others miss and pick up new ideas and concepts quickly. They can incorporate what they previously learned and answer questions about the material. They can sort out inconsistencies with what they learned and correct aspects that they initially misunderstood. For example, when it comes to languages, my sister is brilliant. She writes beautifully and seems to easily find just the right word she needs to get to the point. She picks up foreign languages, with just the right accents, like most of us pick up spare change. Unfortunately, most of us (including me) are not like that.

It was pretty easy for me to find lots of other classmates much smarter than I was. I was smart enough, with good analytical skills, and I possessed an outstanding visual memory, but I could not just go to class, listen to my biology lectures and immediately understand all that I heard. I sometimes got overwhelmed with the material in my courses. I did not know how to

Chapter 7

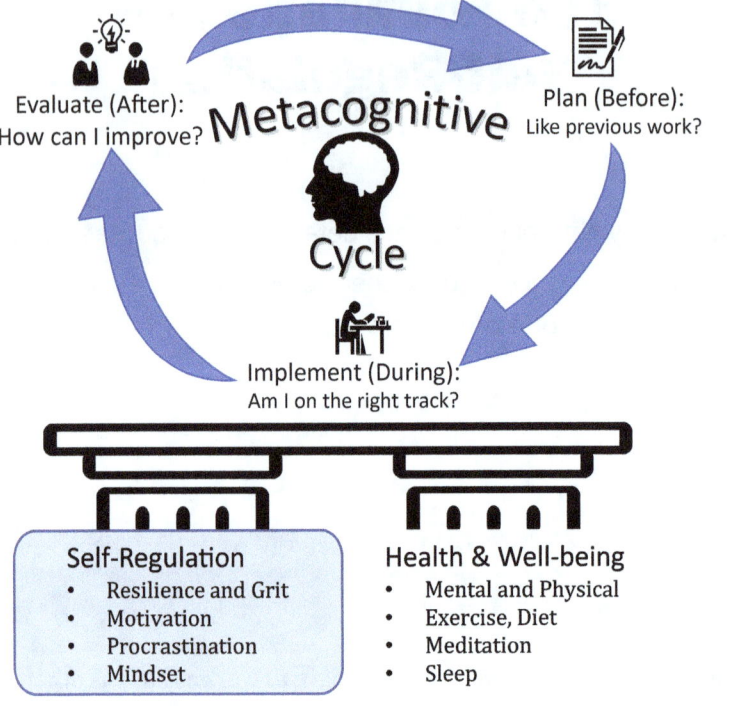

Figure 1. The Holistic Learning Framework: Self-regulation. Unless you have the discipline to study when you need to, no learning strategy will be of use to you.

separate what was important from what was trivial. If something I learned didn't make sense right away, I quickly became lost. I forced myself to go to the lectures, but, for the most part, even as I was standing up to leave the lecture hall, I remembered very little of what was said.

Self-regulation and self-discipline

As I mentioned earlier, I succeeded in school mostly because I had the strength to not give up upon facing initial frustration with a lecture but to get back to study after class. I was able to turn down my friends' invitations to hang out because I was serious about my goals. I wanted to go to medical school (an aspirational goal that I was highly motivated to achieve), so I knew I needed not just to get by with my classes; I had to do well in them. I was convinced that if I worked hard enough, I would be able to achieve my ambitions. I was willing to prioritize my studies and then had the self-discipline to implement my plan.

One of the most critical parts of the Holistic Learning Framework is the two foundational pillars of learning: self-regulation and health & well-being. Of the two, self-regulation has been the most significant aspect of learning for me. Self-regulation allows you to do what it takes to achieve your long-term goals, even when that short-term "I'm too tired to get out of bed" feeling is dissuading you from getting dressed and out the door. Self-regulation requires establishing goals specifically for you, having the right motivation to work for those goals and demonstrating the self-discipline to achieve them.

Self-discipline is not a magical force that some people have or don't have. Self-discipline becomes more manageable when you have correctly aligned your motivations with goals that reflect your values. Misalignment between your learning goals and motivations will require super-human self-discipline to get yourself to study.

Everyone, no matter how smart they are, experiences setbacks with their studies. These setbacks (such as not doing well on an examination or paper) may tempt you to convince yourself that you can't do the work or to come up with excuses, like the teacher is not competent, rather than inspire you to keep working at it. If your goals aren't right, you might end up taking a class that you don't like or where you can't understand why you should learn the material. As a result of these feelings, you are less likely to study, and you will perform worse in your classes, further demotivating you. You can see how this misalignment of goals and motivations quickly becomes a "death spiral" for your learning.

Setting the right goals is a key first step to creating a successful study strategy for yourself. Understanding and developing what motivates you is the next step. Your self-discipline will naturally follow.

> **Motivations Activity Part 1**
> (Approximate Duration: 5 minutes or Longer)
>
> *What are the three most important motivators for you to learn better?*
>
> A)
> B)
> C)
>
> **Aim:** Understand your motivations for learning
>
> **Instructions:** Reflect and write down your most compelling motivators. Are they internal or external?

External versus internal motivation

Like me when I was in college, my NUS undergraduate students all desire to do well in school. However, many of these students are quite different from me in a significant way: when asked the main reason why they want to learn better, their answer is typically to get better grades. They reason that if they get better grades, they will get into better schools, and that will lead to better careers, which will result in earning more money and having a happier life. When I ask why they are taking a particular course, these students often say, "Because I 'have to' in order to fulfil requirements for my major," or "My parents told me I had to," or "I just need the credits to graduate."

What is missing from these statements is consideration of why learning itself is directly valuable to them. They don't often tell me they are curious about the subject, or why it would be cool to learn more about it. Instead, they are externally motivated to learn by rewards outside of themselves, such as the prospect of earning more money or getting a better job or to satisfy their parents' desires. There is little mention of their internal motivations: those desires from within, such as the joy of learning or what gives them a sense of satisfaction.

We all possess a different mixture of externally and internally motivated desires. And some of our motivations are both external and internal at the

The Foundation — Self-Regulation

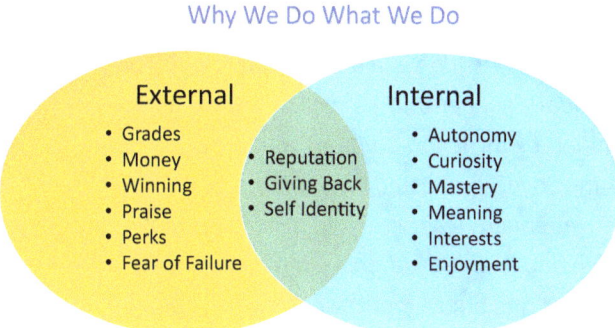

Figure 2. Types of Motivation. Some motivations are both external and internal.

same time.[1] Both types of motivation serve essential functions for us to achieve success. But I find the external reasons that motivate us are not as resilient as our internal ones. External motivations are like your childhood desire to have a toy that you saw on TV and decided you wanted for Christmas. Unfortunately, once you had it, you quickly lost interest in it. It wasn't as much fun as you thought it was going to be. When learning gets tough, external motivation is less persuasive when it comes to encouraging you to keep trying.

Instead, internal motivation is like the gift that you still played with or that sweater you still wore the following Christmas. We have less control over our external rewards; others can decide how much money we earn, or circumstances can change, so these external motivations can become less meaningful to us. The more internally motivated you are to do something, the easier it is to continue to pursue those tasks during those inevitable tough times when things aren't going as well as you hoped.

---

[1] The figure of Intrinsic and Extrinsic Motivation is drawn as an overlapping Venn Diagram because some aspects of motivation include both. For example, enhancing one's own reputation can be quite meaningful to you personally (internal) as well as a value that you hope others appreciate about you (external).

Chapter 7

> "As someone struggling through depression and the university slump, I find it very hard to be consistent. I realized that in my own life, intrinsic motivation is more powerful than external motivation. In secondary school and junior college, I looked for praise and recognition by my fellow students and teachers as my motivation. It was my drive. As a result, I won bursaries and my grades earned [me] the attention I wanted. Now, I'm no longer getting A's or peoples' attention and it isn't an effective motivation. Instead, it [is] my sole demoralizer and stress inducer because the playing field has been narrowed — everyone is smart and the competition is fierce."

Student, Year 3, NUS Faculty of Business

If your primary source of motivation to learn is extrinsic, what will you do when you are no longer in school, and there aren't grades any more to push you? Without enough internal motivation to learn, you might just stagnate with your learning. And there is growing evidence that if you stop challenging your brain to learn, you will lose your ability to think deeply more quickly as you age. The internal drive to keep learning is what will keep you going throughout your life. It is never too late to figure out what truly drives you to learn from the inside.

As a result, the best learners are those that are driven more by internal rather than external motivation. Sometimes, it is our external motivation that gets us started ("I've got to take this course to complete my major"), but the great learners subsequently figure out a connection between what they are learning and what internally motivates them. Sometimes it is not apparent how the information taught in a course ties in with your goals. During a lecture, teachers will sometimes tell you how the material they are teaching relates to what they believe is one of your priority goals. But they are only guessing at the goals that are most important to you. Only you know what are your priority goals and what is externally and internally motivating to you.

Personally, one of my central internal drivers for learning is my natural curiosity. I'm perpetually interested in a variety of topics and particularly interested in knowing more about people. One of the reasons why I studied medicine was that it served my curiosity about how the physical body works, and how the conscious mind thinks. This curiosity has kept me interested in learning throughout my life, even to this moment.

We all possess an innate curiosity. As children, we are very interested in learning more about the world. Somehow, many of us lose that curiosity as we grow up. I wish I knew exactly why some people remain curious, while others lose it. One part of the reason is that we don't spend enough time practicing being curious.

As we progress in school, we are typically told more and more about what and how we should be learning. Our brain naturally tries to conserve rather than expend the energy to think or work. As a result, we tend just to let someone else tell us what to learn. Then we graduate from school, and we have forgotten how to figure out what we should learn next. We are out of practice being curious.

How do you find the aspects of learning that are internally motivating to you? For students, I suggest you complete the following exercise to tap into your internal motivations.

Motivations Activity Part 2
(Approximate Duration: 10 minutes or longer)

Aim: Understanding and connecting more with your internal motivations.

Instructions: Write down one to two paragraphs reflecting on how the courses you are (or will be) taking will make a difference in your life. Especially focus on any course that you find challenging. How is the information taught in the course valuable and relevant to you? What aspects of the material covered in your class are you curious about? What are your internal motivators to take this course?

It might take a little bit of homework on your part to research why learning that subject will be helpful to you. Multiple sources are available to provide clues to the answer to your question. Consider exploring the topic further on the internet, or talking with a more senior classmate, a faculty member or, even better, someone who uses the information you are learning for their job.[2] Clarifying in your mind what you will get out of the courses you are taking will help motivate you to learn the subjects better (Hulleman & Harackiewicz, 2009). The responsibility for this work rests with you![3]

As you think more about what motivates you, it is also helpful to look separately at what demotivates you. It isn't always the opposite or lack of what motivates you. Common reasons for demotivation include reasons we have already discussed on goalsetting: having the wrong goals and not prioritizing between conflicting goals. Most people find their fear of failing to reach their goals to be a frequent reason to feel demotivated. Other causes include being burnt out and exhausted, not feeling in control of how and when we are doing the task (lack of autonomy), lack of challenge, grief over losses in our lives and loneliness.

Demotivations for Learning Activity Part 1
(Approximate Duration: 5 minutes or Longer)

What are your two most important learning demotivators?

A)
B)

Aim: Understand more deeply about what demotivates you.

Instructions: Reflect and write down your most powerful academic demotivators.

---

[2] One of the toughest courses I took in college was Physical Chemistry. It was also a course that I didn't really understand why I had to take, other than because it was a requirement for my major. After writing this chapter, I did an internet search on Physical Chemistry and found some interesting resources that explained the field and why it was important. I wish I had seen these when I was a student!

[3] For a fuller discussion on motivation, I recommend the book by Daniel Pink: *Drive, The Surprising Truth About What Motivates Us*. In this fascinating and fun to read book, Pink describes different drivers of motivation: Autonomy, Mastery and Purpose.

Our natural tendency to overcome feelings of demotivation is to attempt to use more self-discipline to work harder. But this might not be addressing the real reasons for feeling demotivated. One approach to understanding your demotivation more profoundly is to ask yourself the "5 Whys?" As you answer each question, ask another "why" question about your answer.

Example of "Five Whys?" analysis: "I feel demotivated to study in my course because I don't like the subject very much."

1. Why don't you like it very much?
   a. I don't like it much because I'm not doing well in it.
2. Why aren't you doing well in it?
   a. I'm not doing well in it because I'm not spending enough time studying it.
3. Why aren't you spending time studying it?
   a. I'm not spending enough time studying it because I can't get myself to focus.
4. Why aren't you able to focus on it?
   a. I can't focus because I'm unhappy not being able to hang out with my friends and talk about my problems.
5. Why aren't you able to see your friends?
   a. I prioritized studying over hanging out with friends because I wasn't doing well in class. But maybe I'm better off taking a few breaks at planned times to meet up with my friends. It will make me more efficient when I do study.

Chapter 7

> **Demotivation for Learning Activity Part 2**
> (Approximate Duration: 10 minutes or Longer)
>
> 1)
>   a)
> 2)
>   a)
> 3)
>   a)
> 4)
>   a)
> 5)
>   a)
>
> **Aim:** Are you demotivated in any course you are presently taking? This activity helps you understand your demotivation at a deeper level.
>
> **Instructions:** Reflect on one of the academic demotivators you previously identified. Ask yourself a series of "5 Whys" questions to better understand your demotivation. The more time you take to reflect, the more you'll get out of this activity.

We often think our motivational issue is solely a problem of inadequate self-discipline without fully reflecting on what we are really feeling. Understanding and addressing the underlying reasons for your demotivation is the best way for you to strategize on this issue.

Self-discipline is an important factor in learning and like a muscle, it needs exercise. It gets stronger as you use it. If you find that you've messed up and lost your self-discipline, it isn't necessary to beat yourself up about it! We all lose our self-discipline at times! We are typically our worst self-critic and this contributes to our demoralization. Simply forgive yourself, (I try to laugh about how human I can be!) adjust and try again. But this time, work on something slightly easier or take a different approach. Once you accomplish your re-adjusted goals, you can then push harder another time.

Life does not always permit you to learn and do whatever you want. There will be times when self-discipline is necessary to help you achieve something when you can't find a strong internal or external motivation. Sometimes you realize a class you are taking is the bitter medicine that you have to swallow to achieve a higher goal. And after doing it, you might find you really like it after all! However, if you find the need to take a lot of "bitter medicine" to reach your goals, perhaps it is time to readjust your goals rather than force yourself to find the right motivations or increase your self-discipline to learn.

> The "5 Whys?" appealed to me a lot. It brought me the process of thinking deeper [to identify] the root cause of my demotivation factors. It is enlightening for me as I need to confront these issues frequently. Things that demotivated me would be lack of discernible progress, unclear direction and boredom in what I am doing. I have decided to chart down what I have learned and am learning when I do the task. As a result, I can track my progress, clarify with others what I should be learning when I do the task to get a better [sense of the] direction where I am heading.
>
> **Student, Year 3, NUS Faculty of Arts and Social Sciences**

Procrastination

I've held off (procrastinated!) about talking about one of the most significant issues in self-discipline. Everyone procrastinates at times! There are many reasons why we think we procrastinate: being lazy or too tired, or not having enough time, or having other things we have to do. But if we constantly find ourselves unable to find the time to work on goals we prioritize, we are fooling ourselves in some way.

While we try to explain these problems to ourselves with many different excuses, there are two core issues to consider with our procrastination. First, as we already explained, it might be a problem with figuring out our goals! When we have spent time with family, or shopping, exercise, cleaning the house or watching tv, instead of doing the tasks that our goals direct us to do, is it because our inner voice is telling us that these other goals are indeed more important to us at this moment? Alternatively, it could be that the task we are procrastinating about is so unpleasant that we really are willing to accept the consequences of not doing it right away.

The other core reason we procrastinate is that we are struggling with a difficult emotion associated with the task and the short-term answer to dealing with it is simply to avoid it altogether (Sirois & Pychyl, 2013)! It might be a true goal for us, but at the same time, we are scared about some aspect of the task, so we keep putting it off. For me, it was/is: "What if I write this book, and no one likes it?" A thought like that could keep me from even starting a project. And it isn't just fear, but other emotions, such as boredom or frustration, that can also get in the way of our goals.

Even though we avoid the task as a way to comfort ourselves, this solution is only temporary and can even make things worse. This becomes a vicious cycle when we then punish ourselves further for procrastinating: "I'm so lazy!" Our self-esteem sinks lower and for many of us, this negative emotion provokes us to avoid the task further. Forgiving ourselves for having this normal behavior is a good start.

If you are one of those who feel you procrastinate because you are "lazy", this may be a sign that you have not gone deep enough with your understanding of what is really going on for you. Try the "5 Whys?" exercise to see if you can figure how to best help yourself.

A great metaphor that has helped me deal with getting out of this downward spiral of procrastination is to visualize pushing a car that has stopped running. If you have ever had to push a car, you know that it is hardest at the start. But once you get the vehicle in motion and you have overcome the inertia of a car at a full stop, it gets much easier to keep the car rolling. Similarly, I know that once I get started on a task, even one that I am initially highly resistant to starting, it will get easier to keep going once I begin. I just have to start!

The Foundation — Self-Regulation

There are two additional powerful tricks that I recommend to my students to help train their self-discipline, get over their procrastination and get started with their study: "If-Then" statements and setting a routine.

"If-Then" statements

A powerful technique to help your self-discipline is to create "If-Then" types of statements. The "If" is whatever I want to accomplish (like writing this book for an hour). The "Then" is what I get to do if I successfully complete the "If" (usually a treat, for me it is often going for a swim or exercising in the gym). I tell my students not to waste the opportunity to take something you like to do and use it to help motivate you to study. For example, say that you like a cup of coffee in the afternoon. So, instead of that spur-of-the-moment double espresso, chocolate macchiato, with whipped cream, why not decide that you will treat yourself with that same coffee after getting an hour of homework done on your most challenging subject?

Figure 3. Could you use the "If-Then" strategy to get your learning plan or other desired goal in place?

Chapter 7

> *Self-regulation has always been something I've struggled with as I usually press the "Next episode" button on Netflix even though I might have watched several episodes [already]. Using the If-Then approach, I have set trigger points for myself by thinking "if I finish my assignment first, [then] I can watch another episode of Prison Break". Now, I [can] stop between episodes [even with] the suspense of the cliff hanger from the previous episode.*
>
> Student, Year 2, NUS Faculty of Engineering,
> Project & Facilities Management

Having a routine

Writers, performers, artists and athletes have in common the need to be self-motivated to practice. The top individuals in these professions certainly have considerable natural ability, such as height, coordination or intelligence as a start. But it takes more than innate talent to be great. It takes practice. And lots of it. There isn't always someone telling them to practice; they are highly motivated internally to practice. But it doesn't stop there. When you interview these individuals, even they don't rely strictly on motivation to get started. The very best set up a routine to help them. They don't waste any mental effort to think about it or try different ways every day to motivate themselves to do their work. What they do each day is a habit.

Twyla Tharp, the legendary choreographer and dancer, describes in her book, *The Creative Habit: Learn it and Use it for Life,* how she started her routine each day by putting on her workout clothes and hailing a cab in front of her house to go to the gym.

> *"The ritual is not the stretching and weight training I put my body through each morning at the gym; the ritual is the cab. The moment I tell the driver where to go I have completed the ritual. It's a simple act, but doing it the same way each morning habitualizes it — makes it repeatable, easy to do. It reduces the chance that I would skip it or do it differently. It is one more item in my arsenal of routines, and one less thing to think about".*
>
> — Tharp, 2008 —

The Foundation — Self-Regulation

People generally assume that Michael Jordan was one of the best basketball players in the world because of his natural athleticism. While he certainly had many gifts that allowed him to play in the professional leagues, there were undoubtedly many other players who had his height or ability to shoot a basketball. In fact, he failed to make his high school basketball team; there were too many other better players than him. What many feel set him apart from all of the other players was his relentless practice routine, which he named "The Breakfast Club." It started each morning at 5 AM and included weight training and eating well. He never gave himself the choice to miss it because he didn't feel like it. This ritual got him physically and mentally prepared to play.

Both of these two individuals became world-famous in their careers, and they have described their work as their passion in life. Despite that, I find it fascinating that they still needed a routine to help them get started each day and achieve what they wanted in life. In turn, I've tried to develop my writing routine: On my writing days, I wake up early in the morning and head to my neighborhood coffee shop, where I can get a cup of coffee and no one disturbs me while I write for a couple of hours.[4]

It doesn't matter what your routine is: what time of the day, how you start it, if you pair up with a friend or not, but just have one. And practice it. Again, if you find yourself unable to follow the routine, is it because your goals are genuinely elsewhere and not aligned with what you are doing? Is there something that would improve your routine? (Experiment with other times of the day or places.) Similar to the Metacognitive Cycle, it is normal that your routine won't be correct the first few times you try it. So, don't be

---

[4] My routine continues past getting a cup of coffee: I play music on my headphones that serve as background music: not too exciting, not too loud, not too fast. Every 20 minutes I take a 1–2 minute-pause from whatever I'm doing and just have a look around, either out of the window or to people watch. I get up from my chair, head to the bathroom or refill my drink. There are other habits that I have learned to be more effective in my writing. Robert Cialdini, in his book *Pre-suasion* offers an excellent trick for writers who procrastinate. He intentionally stops work for the day at the point where he knows what he wants to say next; he does not write it down. Leaving his work undone at this point provides an additional incentive to get up the next day to work to finish it. Unfortunately, I discovered this habit only in time to help me with the last 2 chapters (Cialdini, 2016).

discouraged if you aren't able to be as self-disciplined as you hoped straight away. Over time, things will change, and your routine might need to change too. Keep trying to find your method until you find one that works for you.

When we don't align our goals with our natural inclinations, we must be especially strategic with our self-regulated learning. For example, most of us find it easy to study our favorite subject. We are already motivated to learn it because we find it particularly interesting, and we find that it comes to us quite quickly. We tend to spend most of our study time on these areas. But what do we do with the topics that are more difficult to get ourselves motivated to work on? Ironically, these are the topics that we generally need to spend more time on because they are typically more difficult for us to learn. But our internal motivation is often less, and as a result, we spend less time on them, rather than more. If we don't thoughtfully and strategically plan our learning, we can easily do things inconsistent with our longer-term goals and values.

Summary: Chapter 7

A solid foundation for learning is a requirement for all of the learning strategies described in this book. The ability to self-regulate (control your emotions and behaviors in order to reach important goals) is one of those foundational skills. It starts by thoughtfully choosing and prioritizing the right goals and understanding the motivations behind those goals. Try to achieve for your learning, the right balance between external and internal motivations. Two powerful techniques to boost your self-discipline include "If-Then" statements and setting up a routine.

References

Cialdini, R. (2016). *Pre-suasion: A Revolutionary Way to Influence and Persuade.* Simon and Schuster: New York.

Hulleman, C. S., & Harackiewicz, J. M. (2009). Promoting interest and performance in high school science classes. *Science*, **326**(5958), 1410–1412.

Pink, D. H. (2011). *Drive: The Surprising Truth About What Motivates Us*. Penguin: London.

Sirois, F., & Pychyl, T. (2013). Procrastination and the priority of short-term mood regulation: Consequences for future self. *Social and Personality Psychology Compass*, 7(2), 115–127.

Tharp, T. (2008). *The Creative Habit*. Simon and Schuster: New York.

Chapter 8

The Foundation — Health and Well-Being

Myth: The harder I work, the smarter I will become, and my grades will keep improving.

Reality: There is a limit to how hard you can work before it begins to detract from your learning.

I have repeatedly stressed in this book that learning still requires, among other things, hard work. However, there is something that you can do to improve your learning immediately, and it may mean less rather than more hard work for you. What? Did you read that right? Yes, and this advice covers one of the main factors influencing my undergraduate students' ability to learn. In fact, it is more important than many of the other learning techniques we have already discussed in this book. Unfortunately, despite the importance, my students rarely think at all about this aspect of their study.

What is this mystery suggestion? Studying optimally means taking better care of yourself, taking a break if you have been working for a long stretch and going to sleep if you are exhausted. As a result of taking care of yourself, you will find yourself better prepared to learn. Good health and a sense of well-being are necessary to maintain the attention and focus required for effective learning. It is so important that I've made this one of the two foundational pillars.

Chapter 8

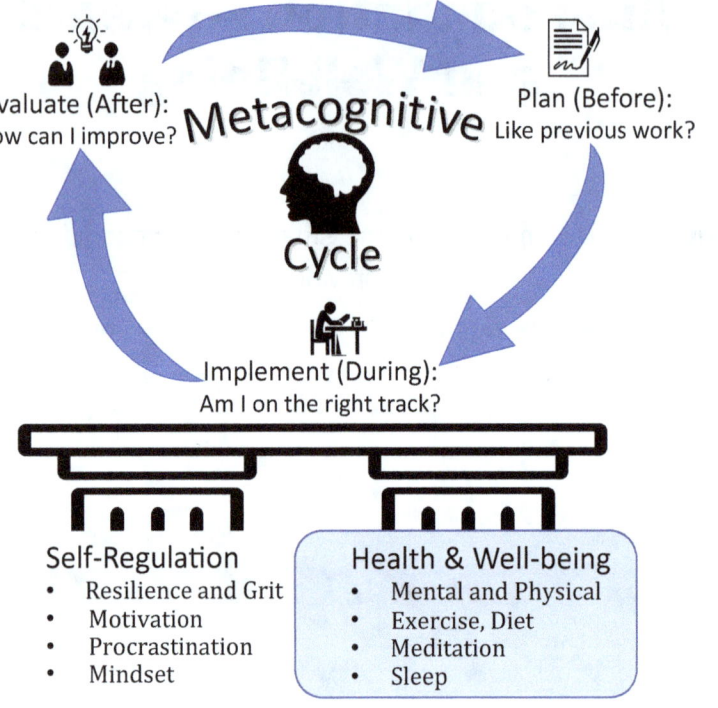

Figure 1. The Holistic Learning Framework: Health and Well-being. You can't study successfully if you are unwell or too tired to learn.

It is easy to forget that our health is one of the most significant factors influencing attention and focus and as a result, better learning. My work each day as a pediatrician reminded me that without good health, my young patients couldn't learn optimally and do well in school. But spending all of your time fixated on your health by exercising, relaxing with friends or meditating doesn't make sense either. You need to find the right balance in your life. That is why proper goal setting is the first step and should serve as a series of guideposts for achieving the right balance for you.

It doesn't make sense to ruin your health to get a good grade in a class either. I know of several extreme cases where students have made themselves

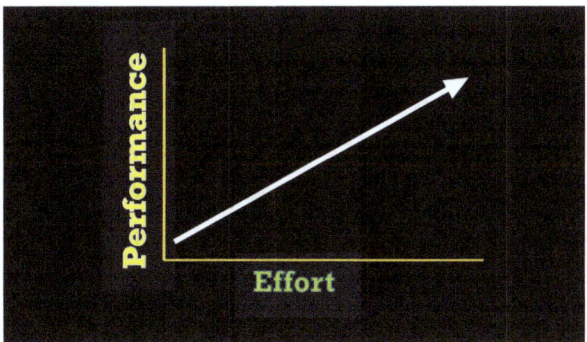

Figure 2. The Relationship between Performance and Effort (the misconception).

sick by working so hard in their attempts to study better. They have a misconception that the relationship between working hard and learning achievement is a straight line:

With this figure in mind, it appears that the more time you spend studying, the more you will learn and the higher grade you will achieve. The amount that can be learned is only a function of how much you can force yourself to study. However, this is a myth.

Instead, our bodies demonstrate a different curve:

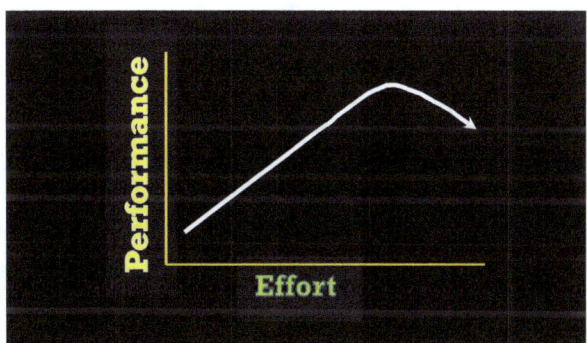

Figure 3. The Relationship between Performance and Effort (the reality).

Indeed, working hard makes a huge difference in your learning. But it only makes a difference up to a certain point. After that, our body begins to burn out and learn less, even as we try to work even harder.

One of my friends is a sports psychologist who helps world-class, Olympic-caliber athletes achieve their training goals through mental coaching that complements their physical practice. He told me that the main problem for these athletes is not convincing them that they need to train harder, but persuading them when to rest and let their body recover. When they over-train, they don't let their muscles recover enough to grow stronger. When they over-train, they find themselves more easily injured, which creates a major setback in their program. For these elite athletes, holding back doesn't feel right to them; it feels counterintuitive to them, but the best coaches know when enough is enough. These athletes need to learn that while they do need to train hard, it must not be so hard as to overtax their bodies.

Learning works similarly. I see students staying up over many nights, trying to cram for an upcoming examination. But at some point, the time spent on studying is no longer efficient, and becomes difficult for any additional information to sink in. If these students had been a bit more strategic and started to study earlier, as well as give themselves a bit more rest in between, they would not waste so much time trying to study inefficiently when they are so tired. When you are physically and mentally well, you are focused and better prepared to learn. Keeping yourself healthy pays dividends when it comes to learning.

Distractions from learning

So, what are the ways in which we can better prepare our mind to receive the information that we want to learn? We live in a world where multiple things are continuously begging for our attention, like a child tugging on our sleeve. We desire to stay up to date on the latest news, idea or fashion, what our favorite celebrity is doing or whatever crisis is going on in the world. However, all of this constant information is overwhelming. We need help to deal with this ever-increasing amount of sensory input coming from smartphones, headphones, computers, watches, etc. Ironically, because we have so many distractions, we then set alarms or notifications to alert us to what we should be paying the most attention to, which adds another layer of sound and vibration clutter vying for our attention.

All of this activity is detrimental to our ability to concentrate and absorb what we want to learn.

There is a well-shared internet belief that our attention span is now shorter than that of a goldfish! While I suspect this is an urban myth, since I'm not able to verify any of the research behind this statement, I'm nevertheless willing to agree with reports that suggest that our minds do indeed have trouble staying focused on a single thought for very long. Our thoughts usually wander endlessly, jumping from our current focus to events in the future or past. Research has estimated that during a typical day, our minds wander almost half of the time! (Killingsworth & Gilbert, 2010; Seli et al., 2018)[1] Since we now live in a world with constant distractions, we have made it even easier for our brain to jump from one thought to another. So much so it may feel eerily strange for you to be in a quiet place without any electronic or other distractions.

The noise around you might be interfering with your study, without you even realizing it. Background speech, whether it is the annoying conversation of strangers sitting next to you or the lyrics of a favorite song playing over headphones, can distract our attention as we unwittingly and subconsciously try to process the words (Lehmann & Seufert, 2017). One study found that listening to instrumental music without lyrics does not seem to have the same detrimental effects on learning as music with lyrics (Avila, Furnham, & McClelland, 2012). I once mentioned to my sister (a trained concert pianist) that I sometimes play classical music in the background while I study. She was horrified and asked how I could possibly concentrate

---

[1] It isn't a trivial undertaking to measure mind wandering for research purposes. It is not simply determining when people have time off or on task, but they have different degrees of attention too. Nevertheless, whatever the exact percentage of time we mind-wander, the point is that we mind-wander a lot! However, all is not lost. Mind-wandering seems to be vital for brainstorming and creativity. Those creative thoughts that come as a result of mind-wandering, will eventually require focused attention to implement successfully. It seems the brain needs different modes to tackle different types of problems.

with classical music playing in the background. Instead, she played smooth jazz while she studied.

Looking more closely at the scientific literature to understand whether to study with or without music is confusing. Some studies indicate that music is distracting and others have found it elevates attention. Factors, such as what you are learning/doing at the time and your personality (introvert vs extrovert), as well as your personal interests, seem to make a difference on the effect of playing music while learning. After reviewing these studies, my advice is if you wish to do so, choose music that is pleasant, repetitive but otherwise not too entertaining to you. Avoid music with lyrics or popular songs that you enjoy. Instead, save those songs for listening before study time or as a treat for your breaks.

Is it multitasking or rapid task switching?

Problematic for our attention and subsequent learning is our compulsion for instant communication with others (such as messaging, phone and video calls) and social media (in the form of Twitter, Instagram, Facebook, etc.). We believe we can be more efficient with our time if we can simultaneously work on different problems in our head, like a computer running several programs at the same time. As we focus on one issue, we convince ourselves that we are addressing others in the background.

Instead, cognitive scientists have found that humans don't solve multiple problems simultaneously but instead rapidly switch from one task to another and then back again. Our ability to process is finite, so even undemanding tasks will undermine complex ones. For example, even talking on the phone or listening to the radio while driving a car will decrease the reaction time it takes to avoid a collision.

A recent study observing students while studying found that a typical student is interrupted or chooses to switch to a different task once every six minutes (Rosen, Carrier, & Cheever, 2013). With each switch, time is lost as the mind re-orients to the new task and has to remember the mental rules that manage it. This lost time is in addition to the time lost getting back to the original task. Speeding up the time it takes to switch tasks has a different cost. The faster this switching of tasks is done in our minds, the more opportunities for mistakes to occur. The differences in multitasking ability between different groups, such as males versus females, or digital natives versus technophobes, are small. And what makes this problem even worse is that we are unaware of the actual impact this rapid task switching has on our learning. Research on our multitasking abilities consistently demonstrates not only that we are weak at multitasking, but also that we are poor judges of the impact of these interruptions on our study (Sanbonmatsu et al., 2013). It appears the more likely you are to believe you are a good multitasker, the more likely it is that you aren't!

Multitasking affects our mental health and is associated with increased anxiety and depression (Becker, Alzahabi, & Hopwood, 2013). However, I think it is a bit unrealistic for us to try to stop multitasking completely; it is normal for the mind to wander about. Although harmful for our immediate productivity when it comes to cognitively demanding tasks, there are times when it may enhance other aspects such as creativity, satisfaction or even maintaining alertness during monotonous situations like a boring lecture or long car drive.

My suggestion for handling multitasking in healthy ways is first to determine which tasks require your utmost concentration. Then schedule times to complete those demanding tasks when you can eliminate as many distractions as possible. Turn your phone to "airplane mode" and turn it back on when you take a break or finish. Plan those concentrated times during the periods when you are most alert and productive. For me, this time is in the early morning. In the late afternoon, when I am more tired, I'll take on less cognitively demanding tasks, like clearing my less critical emails. I'll turn my phone back on and review my messages. I know my mind will wander as I answer all sorts of mail in my inbox, but I just accept that I'll do that and not worry about it too much.

Giving yourself a break

Taking short breaks when studying is helpful to reset your brain, give yourself some time to consolidate what you have learned and help store information in your memory (Ariga & Lleras, 2011; Steinborn & Huestegge, 2016).[2] Even during times set for concentrated focus, I don't stay in front of my computer for longer than 30–40 minutes before taking a break. Sometimes, my break is as short as looking up from my screen and gazing at other people in the coffee shop for a minute or two, before getting back to concentrating on my work. I might work longer at one sitting when I am "in the flow," and I find my brain working well on the task at hand. But as soon as I feel my attention wane, I'll take my break, usually getting up and moving around for a few minutes, or walking to fill my water bottle or heading to the bathroom.

For others, optimizing their learning means balancing their lives with family, religious or social activities. As we previously discussed, as a serious student, it is essential not just to consider your study goals, but to keep perspective on your aspirational life goals as well. By my standard, a balanced, well-lived life includes a wide range of activities that we value, which include caring relationships with others. There is evidence that this balance can help your learning as well. For example, meditation, whether part of a formal religious practice or a form of mental exercise to improve your attention and focus, can help students achieve balance in life and has shown to be beneficial in learning (Ramsburg & Youmans, 2014).

The effect of exercise on learning

As I previously mentioned, I'll use taking a more extended break (going to the gym or for a swim) as my reward in an "If-Then" statement I set for myself ("If I work on my book for forty-five minutes, then I can go for a swim"). Using exercise as a reward has the added advantage of keeping me healthy too. After my exercise break, I'm energized, re-focused and ready to start working again. I feel happier. These effects all contribute to better learning.

---

[2] It appears that a break is even more valuable when working on a cognitively complex task than a more mundane one. And it doesn't seem to make too much of a difference if the break is physical activity (like taking a walk) versus a mental break (like surfing online).

We are starting to understand some direct effects of exercise on learning too. There is growing evidence from multidisciplinary research approaches suggesting that exercise at all age levels can improve learning and academic performance (Hillman, Erickson, & Kramer, 2008). Physical activity may also play a role in maintaining cognitive function as we age, and reducing the risk for Alzheimer's disease and dementia.

The most significant impact on learning for most students: Sleep

For the typical high school and university student, the most significant and most common impact on learning is typically unrecognized: that they live in an epidemic of poor sleep practices. The choices that these students make regarding how much sleep they get have an enormous impact on learning. The percentage of my undergraduate students who are severely sleep-deprived is staggering.

I'm not just talking about the loss of sleep as students cram at the last minute with an occasional "all-nighter" right before their examinations. They are chronically sleep-deprived, especially not getting enough sleep during the weekdays. According to Dr Joshua Gooley, my colleague at Duke-NUS Medical School, the typical student taking my NUS course gets less than seven hours of sleep each night. The average amount of sleep that is considered healthy for these students is at least 1.5 more hours of sleep each night. It is no wonder that these students aren't learning at their peak.

Studying while sleep-deprived has been equated to studying while drunk (Dawson & Reid, 1997). In my opinion, if students are looking for a way to improve their learning without having to study any harder or longer, the best approach is to develop better sleep habits.

What makes their sleep deprivation even worse is that most students are going to bed late at night, and then having to wake up early to attend classes. Dr Gooley has found that our students who are natural "early risers" (they go to sleep early and wake up early) perform better in their university

Chapter 8

Figure 4.   Improving your sleep will have a major impact on your learning.

classes (frequently scheduled in the morning). Unfortunately, this sleep pattern is the minority. On the other hand, the "night owls" who are up late at night are disadvantaged, with their sleep cycle shifted to a later time. Night owls are, in effect, "jet-lagged" during their morning classes. Their bodies are sleepy and tired at the time of the day when they are taking their examinations and hoping that their minds are sharp. Imagine trying to do well on a test when you come off the plane after an international flight. Your jetlag impairs your mind from performing at its best.[3]

With university dorm life seemingly buzzing along most happily and noisily in the hours right after midnight, this forces early risers into a sleep schedule that is not natural for them. And since most school classes start in the morning, students must get up after a few hours of sleep. The demands for our students to pass their courses and fit in a packed study schedule while also juggling their busy social lives is overwhelming. Students are willing to sacrifice their rest because it is less of a priority to them. No wonder our students are suffering from chronic sleep deprivation. And they pay for that with poor learning.

---

[3] There are many published studies which reflect a similar sentiment: students who have a natural body rhythm that reflects the timing of their school classes perform better academically (Haraszti et al., 2014).

As we understand sleep better, we know that it is not merely a time where our minds blank out, only to start up again in the morning when we wake up. Instead, sleep allows our brain to clear out some of the debris that accumulates during the day, using newly discovered channels (Xie *et al.*, 2013). This cleansing is presumably good for the brain.

But we also know that the brain is actively processing information at various times during sleep. Different scenarios are imagined in our sleep and seem to contribute to our learning. Material learned right before sleep seems to be better consolidated in the brain after sleep, and more easily recalled at a later date. Something for those of you who are especially strategic to take advantage of — all it takes is proper planning to wisely choose what to learn right before heading to bed!

Ideas are bounced around during sleep. Many critical insights into scientific discoveries occurred during sleep. Chemist Dmitri Mendeleev found the answer to a logical method of organizing the chemical elements during his sleep. When he awoke from his dream, he wrote down the Periodic Table. The brilliant mathematician Srinivasa Ramanujan recalled that many of his mathematical proofs came to him in his dreams. The expression to "sleep on it" when making an important decision is not just an idle suggestion but potentially has a real purpose.

A lack of sleep has many significant health consequences, which, in turn, further affect learning. For those students who are chronically sleep-deprived, there is a higher incidence of psychiatric disorders such as depression and anxiety, as well as obesity and associated cardiovascular disease and diabetes (Zaharna & Guilleminault, 2010).

Strategies to improve sleep

So, what are some of the things you can do to improve your sleep? Although you probably already know this, it is worth stating that sleeping in a comfortable bed, in a dark, quiet room is an important start. The constant all-night pinging of incoming messages, emails, notifications, reminders and alerts make sleeping in our modern bedrooms more disruptive to sleep

Chapter 8

than our hospital intensive care units. Perhaps the only way many students living in dorms will sleep better is by using eye covers and soft earplugs. Some schools are starting to provide sleeping "pods" in libraries for students to take a nap during the day in a quiet and dark setting!

With our modern lifestyle, having a reasonable place to sleep is not always a given and may need some serious planning and problem-solving to accomplish. Unless you are a physician on call at night, or a government official having to react to an emergency, there aren't a lot of reasons why you need to be immediately available during the night. So, I suggest turning your phone to airplane mode while asleep. The effort you take towards improving your sleep environment will be well worth it, especially in terms of how it will enhance your learning.

Improving your sleep practices is the next most important step. Your body has a natural time clock or circadian rhythm that tries to keep your daily cycle approximately the same each day. So, going to bed at the same time each day makes it easier to fall asleep and stay asleep. You might develop some relaxing routines that you do each night before going to bed instead of watching that heart-pounding action film or drinking Red Bull or a double espresso too close to bedtime. These relaxing routines work to signal the body that it is time to rest.

Finally, carefully consider taking a nap. The afternoon might be the only time that is quiet and peaceful at your house. Your body typically gets tired in the mid-afternoon, so taking a short nap then can help the brain get re-energized again for the rest of the day. However, I suggest only napping for 30–60 minutes, certainly not longer than 90 minutes. If you nap for too long, it can make you quite drowsy immediately after waking up and it will be more difficult for you to get started with your work again.

Despite chronic sleep deprivation, some still find themselves having trouble falling asleep at night, or having a very restless sleep. One reason for this problem is a disturbance in their circadian rhythm. Taking too long a nap or napping too close to bedtime will throw off your natural rhythm. The lack of bright light during the day or too much blue light emanating from your computer or smartphone in the evenings may also challenge your circadian rhythm.[4]

The use of medication for sleep could paradoxically cause sleep problems, especially if misused. Other, more serious medical illnesses can result in disturbed sleep. If you have problems falling asleep, or feel excessively tired during the day and it persists, then you should see a sleep medicine professional for help. Don't self-medicate!

Other health issues

Serious mental and physical health issues will obviously prevent students from learning. The effects of alcohol and drug abuse on health and learning are also self-evident. A full discussion of these health issues' impact on learning is beyond what I can cover in this book. But as this chapter indicates, even less serious mental and physical health issues can have a substantial effect on how we optimally focus and learn.

After telling you so many times in this book that hard work is essential, perhaps you will be surprised that I'm now suggesting that you might do better NOT working so hard. And even though some of these suggestions might involve less work for you, these issues will be among the most challenging things for you to change. It turns out there are many reasons why improving your personal health habits, like better sleep or nutrition, more exercise, etc., is so difficult to achieve. My suggestion is to start with baby steps. Determine what you think is most do-able, like changing the music you listen to while studying, or turning your phone to airplane mode while you sleep. Take time and be patient as you slowly incorporate the other suggestions in this chapter into your life. Even at my age, I'm still trying to bring more wellness into my own life, a little bit at a time.

---

[4] There are software programs that cut the blue light coming from your computer or mobile phone screen or special glasses that cut down the amount of blue light that you see. Some blue light in the daytime might be helpful in regulating your circadian rhythm, but too much late at night can disrupt it.

Implementing all of the strategies I've covered in this book will be overwhelming for almost everyone and not straightforward. Knowing these strategies is easier than implementing any of them. In the next chapter, we'll cover how to bring the information I've given you altogether and develop a learning plan that works to help you achieve your goals.

Summary: Chapter 8

Health and well-being is the other foundational pillar that must be solidly in place for optimal learning. All learners should consider strategies to improve their sleep and health, which enhances their ability to focus while studying. Our bodies have a natural rhythm and times when we can more easily focus. Your learning strategy should take this pattern into account. The right balance of work, rest, social commitments, and other aspirational goals is different for everyone, but achieving this balance will result in better learning.

References

Ariga, A., & Lleras, A. (2011). Brief and rare mental "breaks" keep you focused: Deactivation and reactivation of task goals preempt vigilance decrements. *Cognition*, **118**(3), 439–443.

Avila, C., Furnham, A., & McClelland, A. (2012). The influence of distracting familiar vocal music on cognitive performance of introverts and extraverts. *Psychology of Music*, **40**(1), 84–93.

Becker, M. W., Alzahabi, R., & Hopwood, C. J. (2013). Media multitasking is associated with symptoms of depression and social anxiety. *Cyberpsychology, Behavior, and Social Networking*, **16**(2), 132–135.

Dawson, D., & Reid, K. (1997). Fatigue, alcohol and performance impairment. *Nature*, **388**(6639), 235–235.

Haraszti, R. Á., Ella, K., Gyöngyösi, N., Roenneberg, T., & Káldi, K. (2014). Social jetlag negatively correlates with academic performance in undergraduates. *Chronobiology International*, **31**(5), 603–612.

Hillman, C. H., Erickson, K. I., & Kramer, A. F. (2008). Be smart, exercise your heart: Exercise effects on brain and cognition. *Nature Reviews Neuroscience*, **9**(1), 58–65.

Killingsworth, M. A., & Gilbert, D. T. (2010). A wandering mind is an unhappy mind. *Science*, **330**(6006), 932–932.

Lehmann, J. A., & Seufert, T. (2017). The influence of background music on learning in the light of different theoretical perspectives and the role of working memory capacity. *Frontiers in Psychology*, 8, 1902.

Ramsburg, J. T., & Youmans, R. J. (2014). Meditation in the higher-education classroom: Meditation training improves student knowledge retention during lectures. *Mindfulness*, **5**(4), 431–441.

Rosen, L. D., Carrier, L. M., & Cheever, N. A. (2013). Facebook and texting made me do it: Media-induced task-switching while studying. *Computers in Human Behavior*, **29**(3), 948–958.

Sanbonmatsu, D. M., Strayer, D. L., Medeiros-Ward, N., & Watson, J. M. (2013). Who multi-tasks and why? Multi-tasking ability, perceived multi-tasking ability, impulsivity, and sensation seeking. *PloS one*, **8**(1), e54402.

Seli, P., Beaty, R. E., Cheyne, J. A., Smilek, D., Oakman, J., & Schacter, D. L. (2018). How pervasive is mind wandering, really? *Consciousness and Cognition*, **66**, 74–78.

Steinborn, M. B., & Huestegge, L. (2016). A walk down the lane gives wings to your brain. Restorative benefits of rest breaks on cognition and self-control. *Applied Cognitive Psychology*, **30**(5), 795–805.

Xie, L., Kang, H., Xu, Q., Chen, M. J., Liao, Y., Thiyagarajan, M., ... Iliff, J. J. (2013). Sleep drives metabolite clearance from the adult brain. *Science*, **342**(6156), 373–377.

Zaharna, M., & Guilleminault, C. (2010). Sleep, noise and health. *Noise and Health*, **12**(47), 64.

Chapter 9

Developing, Implementing and Evaluating a Learning Plan

Myth: Once I know how to learn better, I will be able to learn better.

Reality: Knowing about learning is only the first step. It is much harder to implement a plan that improves your learning.

Without a doubt, it takes both intelligence and hard work to learn well. In previous chapters, I emphasized my belief that of the two, working hard is more important than having the natural gift of intelligence when it comes to academic and career success. And, no matter how intelligent you are, there will always be room to grow. However, I think you also understand by now that those two factors are still not enough.

The best learners are strategic learners because they know different ways to optimize their learning. But is knowing how to learn even enough to become a strategic learner? There are at least four necessary ingredients to learning better; doing the first three without the last one will not lead you to learning better:

Chapter 9

1. **Intelligence**
2. **Hard work**
3. **Knowing learning strategies**
4. **Knowing how to implement these strategies**

We have now covered the different learning strategies which make up the building blocks of a learning plan. But it turns out that knowing about how to learn is easier to achieve than implementing this knowledge. Strategic learners deal with the complexity of learning by developing those blocks into a plan. Your plan should consider all elements of our Holistic Learning Framework. Developing your learning plan begins with the top part of our framework, the Metacognitive Cycle. We learned about setting goals that guide your study and putting learning in perspective with the rest of your life goals. Then, using appropriate, evidence-based, proven strategies that optimize learning, you tailor your plan to meet your specific needs and situation.

We then discussed the bottom component of the Holistic Learning Framework. Creating a solid foundation of both self-regulation and health and well-being supports your learning, allowing you to stay on track and follow through with your learning plan. Therefore, attention to your overall health and commitment toward well-being, which includes proper amounts of exercise, nutrition, sleep and rest is a must. Understanding your motivations and how to best keep yourself focused despite the myriad of modern-day distractions is also a part of this foundation.

We need to finish our discussion by returning to the Metacognitive Learning Cycle and covering the final two steps: "Implement" and then "Evaluate." The only way to know how your plan works is to try it out. And after monitoring the implementation of our plans, we must then evaluate them using the "3 Rs": Review, Reflect and Revise. Finally, we describe this process as a cycle because the best strategic learners don't just make a plan, implement, evaluate it and then stop. Instead, strategic learners use the Holistic Learning Framework to repeatedly improve their learning plans over time. They then start the cycle all over again. This improvement cycle should continue throughout your life as a learner.

Developing, Implementing and Evaluating a Learning Plan

Before we complete our discussion and bring all of the elements of the Holistic Learning Framework into our personal learning plan, there are a few other things to consider for your plans. These practical suggestions will make it more likely that you'll have the impact on your learning that you desire.

Brainstorm for obstacles to your plan

Your learning plan will be more resilient if you also carefully consider what obstacles exist to achieving your goals (Oettingen, Mayer, & Brinkmann, 2010). This common-sense strategy asks you not only to visualize the steps to successfully achieve your goals, but also to visualize how you may overcome the issues most likely to disrupt achieving those goals.

A frequent issue that many learners complain about is their lack of "time management skills." However, this term is too broad to be helpful and deeper reflection is required to figure out the real problem to solve this issue. The "5 Whys?" analysis (page 97–98) will help.

Perhaps you will discover that your "time management" issues are the result of a lack of clarity about your priorities and you need to update your goals. Or maybe you are wasting time because you lack focus while studying, and you can't seem to resist the temptation to get on your phone? Then turn off your phone and put it away so you can't see it. Is procrastination the reason for not having enough time to complete your priority tasks? You already know many powerful techniques that you can use to correct the root cause of this issue.

It is not enough to know about evidence-based learning strategies. You now need to do the hard work of figuring out what is limiting your academic success and how you can strategically implement plans that work for you.

Learning with others

Although this book has so far emphasized individual approaches to improve learning, please do not conclude that learning should always be a solitary

Chapter 9

Figure 1. Forming a study group can be helpful, but it must be set up correctly to help, not hinder, learning.

activity. Many students (myself included when I was in college) think that study groups are a waste of time and would rather just study individually instead. The truth is that study groups can indeed be a major time-waster. But they don't have to be; a well-thought-through learning plan should strongly consider working with others. It can complement the individual learning strategies that you have selected for your plan.

The potential benefits of learning in groups are substantial. The group could share questions (from question banks or, even better, written by group members themselves) for retrieval practice. A study group discussion might be the only way for you to identify and resolve any misunderstanding of the material before an exam. Teaching others in your study group what you have learned is another way to increase your depth of processing and deepen your understanding of the material. If you can teach it to others well, then you really understand it!

The other benefit of studying in teams is to exchange thoughts about what are the most important areas to study. The questions that the group develops should focus mainly on those areas. A discussion comparing everyone's opinion about what is the highest priority information to study happens naturally if everyone is responsible for bringing in questions that they believe cover key concepts.

Some students find that being accountable to others by committing to join a study group is just the right motivation they need to keep up with their work. Another aspect that is not always appreciated by students is that learning to become a member in a high-functioning team is a skill that is often not well developed, despite its critical importance in the modern workplace. One of the most important skills you can acquire in school is learning to manage the inevitable conflicts that arise in any group and communicating respectfully with others. These things takes practice! So don't underestimate this side benefit of learning in a study group, even if you don't get a grade for it.

I suggest finding three or four classmates that you think will have similar study goals as you to form a study group. Scheduling a convenient time for everyone to meet becomes much more difficult if too many people are involved. Sometimes, a group decides the best learning strategy is "divide and conquer." While splitting up different topics for each team member can be an efficient way to preview the material or set responsibility for developing questions for retrieval practice, be careful! The major pitfall to avoid with this plan is individuals in the group not understanding all of the materials, only the part they were assigned.

Students frequently have bad experiences with study groups because there is no shared vision determined at the beginning of what the group can and should accomplish. A group can quickly evolve into a social gathering for fun conversation, or a complaint session about the course or the instructor, rather than achieve its intended purpose: to study! Or the study group can end up with one or two members "doing all of the work" and the others just "slacking off." A study group contract or charter is a great way to get everyone on the same page before the study group even starts. Even though it is not necessarily a fun activity, it is much better to agree on ground rules at the start rather than waiting until disagreements surface; by then, it might be too late to save the group.

I've included a sample team contract in Appendix C. Ideally, this document should cover what the group wants to accomplish, and decisions on such things as how frequently to meet, requirements for attendance and expected individual preparedness for each meeting. Roles in the group (such as choosing or alternating leadership, who is responsible for communications, scheduling, etc.) should also be determined. Don't forget to set a time after a few months of working together to review how well the group is doing and if everyone is satisfied.

> Buddy up... this will enhance our learning. Buddying up to build accountability.

Student, Year 2, NUS Faculty of Business

Implementing your metacognitive learning cycle

After strategically setting your learning goals and deciding which learning strategies you want to include (Plan), there is still much work to do. We now return to the Metacognitive Cycle and discuss the second part: Implementation.

What works for one person might not work as well for someone else. The study materials in a humanities class are different from those in the natural sciences, and the examinations for these subjects will be quite different. Therefore, study techniques that work in one discipline might not be as appropriate for other subjects. How do we fine-tune our learning plans in a strategic fashion?

It is difficult to fully anticipate how your plan will work. Therefore, the next step to fine-tune your Metacognitive Cycle is just to get started, no matter how imperfect or incomplete your plan. During the Implementation phase of the cycle, it is important to monitor and note what happens as you implement your plan. Since many of the strategies are counterintuitive to

Developing, Implementing and Evaluating a Learning Plan

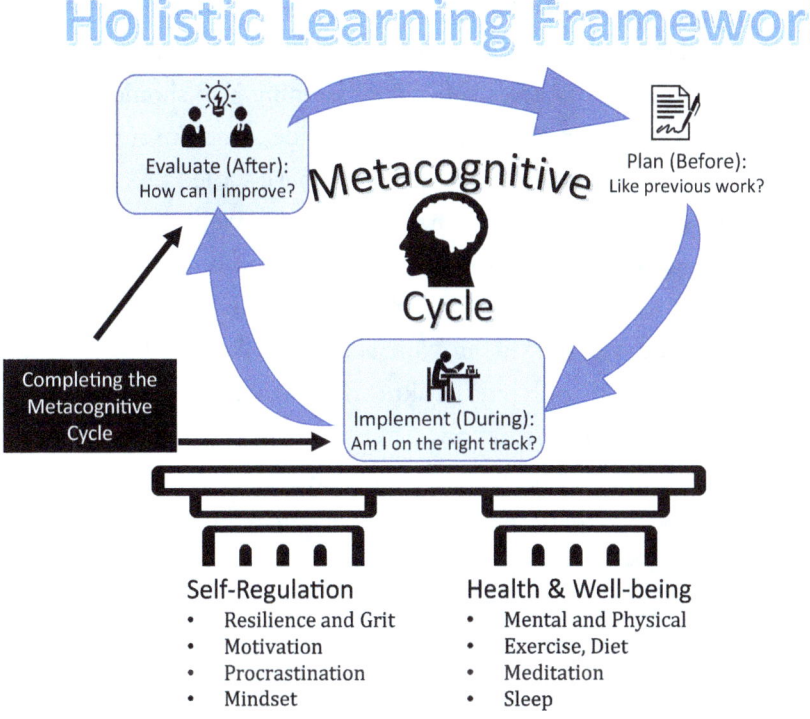

Figure 2. The Holistic Learning Framework: Completing the metacognitive cycle: implementing and evaluating.

what you first thought optimal learning to be, don't be too quick to make major adjustments in your plan. The main reason I've made "Implement" its own step in the Metacognitive Cycle is to make sure you allot sufficient time to this. Give your plan a chance to work and monitor how it makes you feel. You'll have the opportunity to evaluate how the plan has worked for you later, after you have more information about how you've performed using these new study ideas.

Evaluating your metacognitive cycle

The Holistic Learning Framework tries to organize the key, complex factors involved with better learning. Perhaps you have kept notes in Appendix A on the top ideas that you want to try out. It should be obvious now that your cycle must be personalized because each learner has unique natural talents, personal motivations and goals. Since your learning plan should take into account these differences, there are lots to consider. And I'm sure you will want to reconsider many of the parts after you have started.

With all of this complexity, what is one to do? Well, the reason that I'm not willing to prescribe to you exactly how you should study is that no single plan works for everyone. Therefore, it is up to you to figure those things out yourself, using your scientifically based knowledge of learning, and then applying that knowledge to develop a study plan tailored to your specific situation. After creating and implementing a learning plan that incorporates your best ideas about how you should study optimally, the next critical task is to evaluate how well that study plan has worked for you.

Figuring out your learning plan with so many different factors to consider can feel overwhelming. My suggestion is just to get started by taking small steps with your learning plans. In your evaluation, you might realize that a strategy that you thought would be helpful was not realistic for you to implement. Then you will need to revise and reset your plans, using a different strategy or goal.

As mentioned in Chapter 2 on goal setting, people usually make too many goals that are too hard or too easy. You can rarely get a goal that is "just right" the first time. Then, once you find that "just right" goal, it should change as you progress with your learning. The trick is to avoid getting demoralized by not hitting your targets. When we get discouraged, we tend to think either poorly of ourselves or feel the entire exercise of setting goals is a waste of time.

Instead, I suggest that you reframe your thoughts about goals: Rather than seeing them as fixed, immovable targets, see them as something that naturally needs to be continuously adjusted as you learn. As your needs, values and experiences change, your goals should change as well. Start with the expectation that it is unusual to achieve your goals the first time you try and fantastic if you do (at which point you should change them to make them harder). If you don't achieve them, evaluate what happened and revise.

The magic formula for learning

Optimal learning means becoming an expert on how you learn best, experimenting along the way and then adjusting like a rocket ship flying towards its target. I wish I had a simple, magic formula that works for everyone when it comes to how to learn better; it would be a less demanding book to write than this one!

As you proceed on your learning journey, perhaps you will discover areas outlined by the framework that need more thought and planning. Perhaps you will realize your motivation to learn better is not strong enough to even start a learning plan. Or that you need to understand better your negative emotions (boredom, fear of failure, etc.) as you implement your learning plans. Maybe you will misjudge your needs and desires for a social life and, as a result, will go out with friends far too many nights to study successfully. Or you will learn that your study goals aren't really in alignment with the other priority aspects of life that you value more. We rarely get our plan "just right" the first time — there are too many things to consider.

Evaluate: The "3 Rs" — Review, Reflect and Revise

I hope I've convinced you that our holistic approach to learning requires a continuous loop of planning, implementation and then evaluation. Evaluation comprises "3 Rs": Review, Reflect, then Revise. To help you with the "3 Rs", I've included examples of common questions that can drive your self-evaluation:

1) **Review**: What happened when you implemented different learning strategies? Do you have any evidence that you were learning better?

a. "I especially didn't do well in the transitions between learning different subjects and I didn't know how to adjust my study plans depending on the discipline."
b. "I found myself worn down with frequent illnesses that kept me from studying when I wanted to."
c. "I didn't perform as well on the test as I expected, given the amount of time I committed to studying."
d. "Although I did well on this class, I had to cram at the last moment."

2) **Reflect**: Given my observations of my own learning and assessment of how well I learned, are there aspects of my plan that I should think more carefully about?
    a. "When I looked at the actual amount of time I spent studying different subjects, I realized it didn't reflect my goals. I like to study chemistry because I am naturally good at that subject and get a sense of mastery in it, rather than in my physics class, which was much harder for me. But my goal was actually to do better in physics."
    b. "If I didn't rely on cramming for the test, and spaced out my learning more, I would remember more of this material for my next class."
    c. "My learning plan did not reflect differences in my classes: what I found most difficult, what is required, etc."
    d. "After reviewing my performance, I realized I didn't do as well as I planned because getting an A in that class wasn't an important goal as I first thought it should be."

3) **Revise**: How should I best revise my plans to take into account my personal reflections on how I learned? (If you did well in your learning plan, reflect upon what you might do to make yourself an even better learner.)
    a. "I will spend more study time on the subjects that are harder for me, and less time on subjects that are easier; this will allow me to do better in those areas too."

    b. "I would benefit from the additional motivation provided by a study group, so I will find a few other students to work with me next semester."
    c. "I was overly optimistic about what I would be able to accomplish during the holiday period. Next time, I will better anticipate the time I want to spend with my family."

Failure is a great teacher

It is time to share another little secret with all of you. It isn't really a secret, but it feels like one because so few people seem to talk about it. The secret is that everyone fails. Even the most successful person has failed many times. In fact, the more successful and important they are, the more ways they have failed. And I guarantee that their failures have been much bigger than not passing an examination or getting a bad grade on an assignment. Rest assured, failure is a normal part of life.

Nevertheless, these experiences of learning failure can stir up enough fear that it creates significant procrastination or even complete avoidance for some. These emotions can keep you from achieving your goals. And, yes, if you are wondering, as I'm sitting here writing this book, I am indeed worried that no one will read it. Or, even worse, that there will be a long list of readers writing scathing reviews saying how bad this book is. How embarrassing that would be!

What separates out those who are successful from those who are not is not that the former do not fail. It is that they have learned to congratulate themselves for trying, accept their failures as part of life and, most importantly, have learned as much as they can from these failures. They have figured out that they learn more from their failures than from their successes. They have learned what works well for them and what doesn't. Although I'm sure they were disappointed when they failed at something, there wasn't a need to beat themselves up over it (at least not for too long!). They have learned to treat themselves as they would treat their best friend.

They can be comforting but honest with themselves. In doing so, they don't miss the opportunity to learn from their mistakes and failures.

Creating your personal learning plan

In our undergraduate class at NUS, we ask all of our students to put together a formal learning plan based on their aspirational and SMART goals. We ask our students which study techniques they should apply to their learning and put together a study calendar, which they use to schedule their preparation for the other classes they are taking. After they implement their study plan, we also ask them to reflect on how the plan went and to share that reflection with course instructors and teaching assistants for comments. They then practice revising their plans and resubmit this to us. Each stage of the Metacognitive Cycle is briefly documented in their learning plan.

This assignment is a required part of the class, but it is meant to be entirely for our students' benefit. We don't grade their learning plan, but only try to make suggestions to our students and be of help. It gives us the chance to correct any misunderstanding students still have around the material covered in class and provide additional learning ideas that they can use for their plans. It takes students some time and effort to think about how they learn, reflect and then commit to some of these strategies by writing down a learning plan. We ask them to practice reviewing and revising their plans to guide their preparation for their final examinations.

There are many ways to develop and record your learning plan, and I encourage you to develop your own methods. I have included in Appendix D an example of the formal learning plan we use for our students, along with a few instructions to further guide you. If you find this format helpful, a template for this learning plan is available for download on our website (www.strategiclearn.org under "Resources/Downloadables").

Although students in our course go through a formal process of creating a learning plan, we don't necessarily suggest that they continue to do this plan the same way after the class is completed. For some students, they find it important

Developing, Implementing and Evaluating a Learning Plan

to write their plan down, precisely calendaring which specific study topics they will cover at specific times and when they have in-class sessions, faculty office hours, group study work, etc. Some will even describe in their calendar the different techniques they want to employ at different times, such as spacing their learning or retrieval practice. They might note where they want to study and when they plan their breaks. These extensively documented learning plans make it easier for them to more completely reflect on how they prepare for their classes and maximize their study efficiency. They journal their learning reflections as the semester progresses, so they don't forget. These activities help keep these students organized and fine-tune their learning.

However, after they complete the class, most of my students no longer include this amount of detail in their learning plans. The approach for most students who are learning successfully is to continue to do the things they have always done and add one or two ideas that might help them further. These students will review the Holistic Learning Framework to remind themselves of all of the many different influences on their learning, then informally and very quickly evaluate how they have done with the "3 Rs": Review, Reflect and Revise. This literally can take as little as a few minutes at a time and usually occurs at the point they receive their course grades. They do the "3 Rs" on the fly and decide what they will do differently to improve their learning. Others find it useful to continue writing out their formal plans, even discussing them with their teachers or mentors. I strongly suggest this more formal detailed approach if you are looking to significantly change how you learn.

> *"In preparation for battle I have always found that plans are useless, but planning is indispensable."*
> — US President Dwight Eisenhower —

Students throughout their learning lives should not worry about whether their learning plan is formal or informal, especially since it is something that should be frequently updated. What is more important than the actual learning plan is the planning itself. With the Holistic Learning Framework as a guide,

Chapter 9

I hope you now have an overall learning strategy and a repertoire of techniques you can use to improve your learning. If you are looking to dramatically improve your learning, you will no longer be stuck studying in the same way and somehow expecting things to turn out differently. If you don't initially improve your learning, you don't have to give up because you don't have alternative strategies to try instead. The story you can now tell yourself is not that you just aren't smart enough and you would be better off not trying, but rather, you just haven't quite found the right way to study that works for you. While your new plan may or may not help you, I am confident if you continue to experiment, taking small steps along the way, you will find what does work for you.

The responsibility for better learning falls on your shoulders, the learner, rather than on the teacher. But I'm not ready to let teachers and our educational systems completely off the hook when it comes to their roles in student learning. I've saved the final chapter to cover what teachers should be doing to help you to learn better, and what you can do if they aren't.

Summary: Chapter 9

Strategic learning requires more than knowing how to best study. It involves having the skills to implement your plan. It is much harder to implement a learning plan than most realize. Tips such as brainstorming for what could go wrong with your plan or working in a study group might help. After implementing your plan, the next important step is to evaluate and reflect on how to improve it. Don't be discouraged that this is a never-ending cycle! Great things take time to achieve.

Reference

Oettingen, G., Mayer, D., & Brinkmann, B. (2010). Mental contrasting of future and reality. *Journal of Personnel Psychology*, **9**(3), 138–144.

Chapter 10

Modernizing Education to Learn Better

Myth: These new classroom formats are just the latest fad. I still think a great lecture is the only way to learn.

Reality: Students learn best in classrooms that incorporate active learning and other learning science-based principles.

"Yet many education systems in developed and developing economies alike still rely heavily on passive forms of learning focused on direct instruction and memorization, rather than interactive methods that promote the critical and individual thinking needed in today's innovation-driven economy... These outdated systems limit access to the skills needed to drive prosperous economies and pose risks for global productivity. According to one recent estimate, as much as US$11.5 trillion could be added to global GDP by 2028 if countries succeed in better preparing learners for the needs of the future economy" (Elhussein, Leopold & Zahidi, 2020).
— World Economic Forum Future of Education —

Despite persistent calls over the past several decades for education to transform to accommodate the considerable changes in our modern world, it has not exactly achieved smooth progress. The slow change has not been because of disagreements about the need for change. It is easy to recognize the rapid pace at which new technologies, skills and processes available to solve problems are developing. These require the workforce to learn or risk quickly becoming outdated and replaced. In many of the new "digital innovation" companies, seniority from having a long, committed career with a company or industry is often seen as a handicap, rather than an advantage.

Traditional thinking has been that learning occurs during the time between kindergarten and high school; for a few others, it continues through college before entering your career. Now, we need to change that mentality to one where we must continuously learn over our lifetime, no matter the job or profession. Never before has it been more evident that if you aren't continually learning, you are getting left behind.

Lifelong learning is necessary because technological innovations and skills are not the only things that are rapidly changing. The discovery of new information has also developed at a rapid pace. In 1944, the dean of Harvard Medical School, Dr Charles Sidney Burwell, told his incoming class of medical students that "half of what we are going to teach you is wrong and half of it is right. Our problem is that we don't know which half is which." This statement remains true to this day. Perhaps it is a good thing that we tend to slowly forget almost everything that we learn, and, as a result, our brain updates itself by learning and remembering new truths.

The ability to instantaneously look up information on the internet has decreased (but not eliminated) our needs for the rote memorization of large amounts of data or facts. As a result of these changes, there is now an increasing emphasis on learning a different set of skills, referred to as the 21st Century skills: Communication & Collaboration, Critical Thinking & Problem-solving, Creativity and Innovation.

The lecture as the sole or primary educational teaching strategy is certainly not sufficient for the needs of today's learner. Just as it is evident that we cannot teach people to play the piano by telling them how to play, we can't just tell our students how to perform these 21st Century skills and expect them to do it. We need to find ways to incorporate these skills into our educational processes so they can practice them and get feedback on how they are progressing. And as we have learned, if students practice deliberately, with goals in mind and immediate useful feedback, they will learn well.

How should education change?

The tough question to answer is how exactly education should change. I believe that the science of learning should guide these changes. Over the past several decades, research scientists have learned quite a bit about how people learn best. Unfortunately, our modern teaching practices still fail to utilize very much of the scientific knowledge covered in this book. Although it is heartening that changes in our educational system are happening, the teaching methods based on scientific evidence seem to be moving only at a snail's pace.

Teaching in the modern classroom is very complex, and implementing or avoiding a single pedagogical approach won't provide the solution. Contrary to what many believe, learners attending lectures are not necessarily always learning passively. The best lecturers have always aimed to engage their audience and make them actively think while listening.

When I think back on my most memorable learning experiences, many of them were great lectures by my professors. I still remember some of them decades later. One particular talk I attended was by one of the world's foremost experts on fruit flies. He gave a lecture to a group of students, many of whom were not primarily interested in science. I still remember him prancing about on stage dripping with sweat as he passionately described how these tiny insects slept. He kept the entire room spellbound with his stories and brought this otherwise esoteric subject to life for many people in the room. He received a standing ovation at the end of his talk. Yes, even during a lecture on fruit flies, he made his students think about their own lives. I wish I were as talented a lecturer as he was.

Chapter 10

More than a few times, I've been accused of saying that lecturing is "educational malpractice." That accusation is only partly false. As an educator, I still value a great lecture, primarily when used to inspire, convince and summarize. And this is especially true when great speakers like my fruit fly professor lecture. However, I don't see the lecture as the best way to convey the massive amounts of information that faculty often expect students to remember, especially given the reality that most of us do not possess the same ability to lecture as my professor. Was the fruit fly lecture significant to me? Definitely. Did it help me think and shape my career in science? Definitely. I still remember to this day how inspired I was by his words. Do I remember the facts this professor told me during the lecture? Well, not really. That wasn't the point I took away from his lecture.

Medical school is an extreme example of an educational curriculum that presents tremendous amounts of facts for students to learn. As the volume of information thought necessary for a physician to practice medicine grew over time, faculty responded by just giving more lectures with increasingly detailed facts and, frankly, less inspiration. We now recognize that learners typically take away from most talks only a handful of the most essential points, which usually amount to less than what they can count with one hand. We should admit to ourselves that our attention in a lecture fades in and out, generally focusing most intently on the first and last few minutes of the talk. And for most of our modern learners, they learn even less in a lecture theater because while they are listening to their instructor, they are simultaneously responding on social media and playing computer games using their phones and laptops.

The best teachers remember how hard it was to learn

What makes a great teacher? From the information presented in this book, you now know that I believe great teachers make students do more than just memorize the material. They ask all students to do the harder work to deepen their understanding of the material. They don't just spoon-feed students, even when requested; they know why students say, "Just tell me what I need to memorize for the exam," and why doing that isn't as helpful to them as they think. They make students work just hard enough to learn, rather than making it easy.

However, some misinterpret this statement to simply mean: "Teachers should just make it hard for students to learn," and use it as a justification for not teaching well. My comment is not an excuse for teachers who don't thoughtfully put together an educational program for their students. I've heard this from a teacher: "Since research shows that students benefit from poor teaching, why put in the work to teach well?" Instead, the opposite is true: The best teachers put in lots of effort to purposefully make learning just hard enough to optimize learning. Their students learn well because of their conscious teaching efforts, not despite them.

When I think of great teachers, I find their lessons are like best-selling video games. Video game designers deliberately construct their game so that once you master a particular level (or skill set), it bumps you to the next level. You get rapid feedback in a video game when you haven't done something right (your car crashes, your tanks are destroyed, your points stop accumulating). If a game is too hard, people get frustrated and stop playing. If it is too easy, they get bored and stop playing. The successful games have figured out the "Goldilocks" window of getting things "just right." The best teachers do this as well; they don't make things too easy or too hard for their students.

I have observed that the more expertise people get in a particular area, the harder it is for them to remember how difficult it was for them to learn that same material when THEY first encountered it. They have also forgotten how easy it is to forget what they learned! I see the best teachers as empathetic with their students, knowing what confuses them and what pieces of information can help them understand and remember.

The other thing that top educators possess is an extensive toolkit of teaching strategies. They can pull out the right tool for the specific type of learning needed. They don't try to use a single tool to teach in all situations but tailor their programs to student learning goals. Thankfully, education has identified many different types of teaching approaches that allow teachers to introduce new and more active forms of instruction into the curriculum, incorporating additional requirements for students to self-direct their learning.

New approaches to teaching (such as a flipped classroom) and the learning sciences

After reading this book, you will better recognize how many of the learning principles covered fit well with some of the newer strategies used to teach, such as the flipped classroom or collaborative learning formats such as team-based learning or problem-based learning.[1] These techniques require students to prepare before rather than after the classroom experience. The teacher then constructs the classroom experiences not to repeat what they learned before coming into the class, but to complement it.

These in-class experiences require students to think more deeply about the material, apply them to other problems, critically analyze their logic, and determine their generalizability to different situations. These activities would be challenging for faculty to include during the traditional lecture format. The possibilities for in-class, active learning experiences are limited only by the imagination of the teacher.

For many, modernizing education means using technology better inside and outside of the classroom. Technology has undoubtedly increased the opportunities to learn outside of school with modern internet-based learning systems that can deliver a curriculum at any time to students worldwide. Technology has the potential to move learning from the efficient "classroom as a factory model" (where all students learn the same thing, at the same pace, at the same time, in the same way), to one which "personalizes" learning to

---

[1] When I started at Duke-NUS Medical School, we decided to implement team-based learning (TBL) as our instructional strategy. One of the main justifications for TBL was its alignment with the science of learning. We were one of the first schools in the world to successfully use this pedagogical approach for our entire pre-clinical curriculum. Our educational success led to similar initiatives at other schools in Singapore and back at Duke University in the US.

the needs of individual students. Much work remains on how technology can solve the Goldilocks'/learning sciences problem of providing an education to each student that is not too hard, or too easy, and just right at any particular moment in time. Since we have already figured out how to do something similar with our video game technology, I'm confident this personalization will eventually find its way into our teaching and learning practices.

In the introduction, I touched on the differences between memory and learning. Some students can do well in school using memorization skills since this is what is generally tested by teachers. But to do well in your career after school, it is what you have learned, not what you have memorized, that is important. Teaching approaches that emphasize learning, not just memory, will better prepare students for the future.

Also, I believe these approaches should incorporate elements of collaborative learning, where students work together in some fashion to solve problems. Our modern society sometimes allows for a lone person working remotely to contribute in meaningful ways. However, most of us will join the workforce as part of larger teams of people. In this setting, the experience of working collaboratively with others will be a critical key to success.

Most of us have had a few unfortunate experiences working in teams. In these poorly functional teams, we learned very little and achieved few productive outcomes. If we correctly construct collaborative learning experiences in school, all students benefit and learn the teamwork skills that prepare them for our modern workforce.

We used to think that teamwork skills are simple and don't require any instruction. We need to re-think that assumption. Look at any successful professional sports team, with outstanding and talented individual players who have trained in their sport for most of their lives. Their success still relies on a great coach to give them feedback on how to work with others while taking the best advantage of their strengths. Our teachers must do the same with their students in the classroom.

Now that you understand more about the science of learning, some of the latest ideas about education now should make more sense to you.

Chapter 10

Figure 1. Robert Kamei is teaching a class using collaborative learning techniques for deeper processing and greater understanding.
Source: Ministry of Education, Singapore. Academy of Singapore Teachers. All rights reserved.

This understanding is essential for you to take full advantage of these new pedagogical approaches and to build your learning plan around them.

Why are we so stuck on tradition in education?

Despite strong evidence regarding how we learn best, there are several reasons why our school systems haven't been very nimble with our educational programs. First, teaching students in ways that incorporate scientifically-based learning concepts turns the entire idea of "teaching" on its head. Teachers say: "My teachers taught me using lectures since early in grade school. So how can it be wrong?" "I prefer to run the class where I'm in charge. Students should just sit and listen." Unfortunately for these individuals, times have changed.

Both instructors and students often strongly believe in the myth that teachers should make it as easy as possible for their students to learn. Some teachers have told me, "Unless I tell them myself, they won't ever learn it." I wish I had a penny each time a student told me, "Just tell me what I need to memorize for the test; why do we have to do any of this extra work to apply what we know?" If the only outcome of their learning is to pass a test, this is a reasonable question to ask. If they want to understand this material and potentially use it in their careers, they benefit from this extra work processing what they have memorized.

Secondly, these new teaching practices place more responsibility for learning on the student's shoulders rather than the teacher (the expert). Ironically, at the same time that students are complaining that their teachers are offloading their work onto them, their teachers are saying, "Where will I find the time to figure out how to teach differently?" And "If I teach differently, how will I do it?"

It is much harder to create active learning experiences and more challenging to facilitate it in the classroom than to give a lecture. With all of the time pressures facing all of our teachers at all levels of instruction, it is understandable there is tremendous resistance to change. I believe that teachers would do the work and find the time to teach differently if they knew their work would make a difference. We also need our educational leaders to understand and value how people best learn; without their complete buy-in, any teaching changes will be challenging to implement successfully.

However, a shared experience of brave educators trying to stretch beyond traditional teaching practice is that they take terrible risks with their careers. There is much less danger staying with the status quo. A faculty member once confronted me after I had implementeded a new and more active form of teaching into our school: "You don't understand education, and you don't know what you are doing. Students are begging me just to give them a lecture on what they need to know. There is so much to learn; they don't have the time to do anything else, especially the additional things you are asking them to think about."

Students (and their parents) who believe in the learning myths highlighted in this book often criticize teachers who try to change education. I certainly understand why students worry so much. They believe that their school grades (rather than what they learn) are critical for their future success in life. Students feel that their teacher's job is to feed them information that they can digest, assimilate, and then use to score well on their tests of memorization. They accuse their instructors of not doing their jobs when they are required to self-direct their learning or asked to process further the information delivered to them.

Students correctly interpret these innovations as their teachers making it harder for them to learn. As this book points out, what they misjudge is that when teachers successfully implement "make it harder" into their teaching program, it can be better for both student rote memorization and understanding.

Unfortunately, most teachers and students don't know the information presented in this book. I believe that everyone (not only students and teachers but also parents and educational administrators) need to better understand the learning sciences to change education. After reading this book, I sincerely hope you now understand which innovative teaching programs to support and why. But just as it isn't always evident to learners what is a good learning experience, I must state that the same is true about the new ways of teaching (Hessler, 2018). Even if a new teaching approach is based on our understanding of the science of learning, it might not necessarily be suitable for your classroom. What works in one setting might not work in another. We can't rest; we must still carefully and continuously evaluate our teaching programs for optimal learning.

What can learners do if their teachers aren't willing or able to change their classrooms?

I must admit that the first answer to this question that comes to my mind is: Give this book to your favorite teacher or educational administrator!

I'm hoping that many of the readers of this book are teachers. Like everyone else, teachers need to learn more strategically too. Furthermore, when they learn about learning, they also help their students learn. Although this book focuses on how to learn, for more information about educational research around teaching better, take a look at Appendix E.

As we have discussed, our brain is wired to conserve energy where it can, which means our natural tendency will be to try to be lazy or find shortcuts to our tasks. It is human nature to want to be passive rather than active with our learning. I find the best students have figured out that they have to overcome that tendency and have found that working hard is a good learning strategy despite the temptation just to pursue the minimum amount of work.

If students find themselves in an old-style "traditional classroom," not all is lost. The student can use the suggestions in this book to turn that traditional, passive, lecture-based teaching into an active learning opportunity for themselves. For example, the learner can read the required chapter ahead of class instead of only reviewing it after class is over. When the lecture turns to that information, they have had a head start organizing that material in ways that make additional connections and encoding that memory easier.

As you listen further to that lecture, you can ask questions (either by raising your hand or silently writing it in the margin of your notes). Or try to take notes using your own words (or even draw pictures or mind maps) rather than writing down verbatim what the teacher says. Take the time to meet your professor during office hours.

You can also organize a study group. The time used to discuss the material in study groups will deepen your understanding, especially when you help others understand. As one of my professors used to say, "To teach is to learn twice."

Learning in the virtual classroom

Besides advances in information technology, the other significant impact on education has been the recent worldwide pandemic caused by the COVID-19 virus. As I write these words, we are still in the midst of the outbreak, with no end in sight. At least for now, the traditional large classroom no longer exists. Undoubtedly, many future articles will discuss how this life-changing event has forced educators to respond and to what extent we will return to the traditional classroom after this has passed.

The first electronic books, "e-books," created several decades ago, were no more than just images of book pages seen on the computer screen rather than on paper. There was initially little to distinguish the two formats except that e-books provided students greater access to the written literature than their physical counterpart. E-books have subsequently evolved and now link sentences to other information within the book itself, and to other links found in the internet. There can be embedded video, places to keep notes, and track progress and understanding. Similarly, as faculty rushed to make their traditional classroom virtual, a comparable phenomenon resulted. Faculty who previously gave passive lectures, just delivered these same lectures over video conferencing platforms, with students passively listening from their computers. However, for faculty wishing to provide a more active learning session, the virtual setting made it harder for them to engage with students. They could no longer easily see confusion or boredom on the faces of their students. They didn't have the skills to easily set up collaborative, small group online learning activities.

Faculty overwhelmed with quickly converting their curriculum for online delivery also had little time or energy to help students with their problems learning online. Students did not know how to raise questions to faculty or have the opportunity to lean over and ask another classmate a quick question. Since they lacked the opportunity to make friends in the classroom, they missed opportunities to learn collaboratively. Their homes sometimes lacked adequate places for them to attend these virtual classrooms or to study. Students learning in the "comfort" of their homes were not used to managing the distractions of their homes. Some lacked tools to self-regulate their learning at home.

Faced with these new learning challenges, the students who successfully coped were the ones who had the skills and solutions to adjust to this new environment rapidly. These students already had a strategic approach to learning. For example, if they found themself having a hard time getting started on their homework with all of the distractions at home, they knew how to use the "If-Then" technique to beat their procrastination. Perhaps some students frustrated with trying to understand their online video lectures realized they could use the strategy of pre-reading and mind-mapping the material before class. They could challenge themselves to raise at least one "chat" question during class time. Other students recognized they could make up for the loss of the personal interactions that naturally occur with attending class by forming a small in-person study group.

Using the tools you learned from this book, you now have tools and a comprehensive approach that will serve to guide you with whatever learning challenges, COVID-19 or otherwise, that you face.

Lessons from my father

When I think back to what it meant to be a learner in the past, the first person I think of is my father, who passed away several years ago. He was a role model for me as a learner. While I'm missing many details of his learning path, I'm fortunate to have heard a few stories from him. From the perspective of an admittedly proud son, I think my father was the most brilliant person I have known. He grew up on a farm, the first and only member of his family to go to college. His six brothers and sisters frequently complained when he studied for school since it took time away from farming chores. As a result, he had to hide from them whenever he read a book.

At the start of World War Two, he and his family, along with 120,000 other Japanese Americans living on the West Coast of the United States, were accused of being disloyal. They were removed from their homes and forced to live in internment camps built in remote areas of the country.[2] My father was a teenager at the time. His family ended up in a camp located in the desert of Arizona. Since there weren't always high school teachers available in the camp, he told me he often had to read the textbook before his math class and then taught what he learned to his schoolmates.[3]

---

[2] For those curious to learn more details about the Japanese American Internment camps, perhaps the best starting place is the website by the Smithsonian Museum: https://americanhistory.si.edu/exhibitions/more-perfect-union-japanese-americans-and-us-constitution.

[3] When I first heard my dad tell me the story about how he had to teach his classmates their math lesson each day, I felt sorry for him. However, I have come to understand that this was actually a gift to his education and I feel that it was a great factor contributing to his academic success. If you can teach something to others, you have learned that material on a very different, deeper level.

Chapter 10

When World War Two ended, he joined the US Army as a medic. While serving in the military, he applied to one of the best science and engineering universities in the country, the California Institute of Technology (also known as Caltech). Unfortunately, because his military post was overseas, he was unable to take their required entrance examination. Caltech made an exception and allowed him to take the exam at a later time. Despite him having only a makeshift, unrecognized high school education and taking a substitute entrance exam, he was admitted by Caltech as a student.

Caltech's gamble on my father paid off, and he graduated with Bachelor's and Master's Degrees in Chemical Engineering. His education taught him to think using what is known as first principles. First principle thinking has been around since the time of Aristotle. The technique solves complicated problems by breaking them down into their most fundamental elements or assumptions. After graduating from school, my father began a career in the aerospace industry. His work involved cooling airplane cockpit instruments, keeping them from overheating and breaking down. He solved those problems using his knowledge of the basic first principles of thermodynamics and heat transfer.

During his career, there was no internet to search for information on the latest techniques and designs. It was not possible to simply use solutions found elsewhere to solve the problems he faced at work. On rare occasions, he went to work-related conferences, but as is the norm in private industry, most of his work was closely held as company secrets and not widely shared with others. While he undoubtedly learned many new ideas throughout his career as an engineer, he had fewer opportunities for continued formal education than we have today.

He worked closely with colleagues, brainstorming with his team and then testing those ideas in the lab. His brilliance was in his ability to think clearly and solve problems using the first principles that he learned in college, instead of recalling minute facts that he might have memorized. There was no internet where he could quickly find out how others had solved similar problems and choose the answer that best fit whatever problem he was trying to solve.

Today we have a great challenge to change education; and my father's learning story and career have shaped my beliefs about education. We are lucky to have what he didn't: an abundance of information, readily available to us at any moment. We have countless online courses we can take to keep us up to date on the latest innovations. We have communication networks that allow us to easily reach out and speak with other experts in our field. But as we incorporate these and other technical advances to change education, we shouldn't forget the best parts of how we were educated in the past.

We must learn how to apply the fundamental principles of what we learn as well as recall them. We shouldn't answer questions in school with "copy and paste" answers found elsewhere on the Internet, no matter how attractive and comfortable it is for students to do that. The most successful workers in the future will have fine-tuned their skills in school by practicing the hard work of thinking of new solutions. They will not be satisfied with merely searching for and finding someone else's answer to their problem.

Summary: Chapter 10

Students in higher education have considerable influence on the success and failure of teaching innovations; their opinions matter! Knowledge of the learning sciences presented in this book can guide students to advocate for teachers to use more evidence-based educational practices in their classrooms. Understanding the scientific basis for these innovative teaching approaches will also allow the learner to get more out of these practices when they are used in their courses.

The strategic approach described in this book can help students adjust to any learning challenges they face, such as adapting to the virtual, online learning environment and subsequent "education new normal" resulting from the recent COVID-19 pandemic.

Chapter 10

Reference

Elhussein, G., Leopold, A., & Zahidi, S. (2020). Schools of the Future: Defining New Models of Education for the Fourth Industrial Revolution. Future Skills Centre, Canada. Retrieved from https://fsc-ccf.ca/references/schools-of-the-future-defining-new-models-of-education-for-the-fourth-industrial-revolution/.

Conclusion

Final Thoughts on the Power of Thoughts

Myth: My thoughts about my ability to learn aren't important. It's all about my intelligence and learning plan.

Reality: Your thoughts about yourself can have a significant impact on how well you learn and perform in school.

If you have spent the time to read this book up to this conclusion, then you are probably convinced that a strategic approach to learning will improve your academic performance, above and beyond your natural learning talents. Besides your natural ability, your willingness to work hard, and implement study techniques to learn better, there are other powerful influences on your learning. There is a large body of convincing research demonstrating a variety of psychological influences on your ability to learn better (Yeager & Walton, 2011).

I can relate directly to these research findings because of an incident that occurred during my freshman year in college. I took an introductory physics class that was required by my major, and the experience dramatically changed my perceptions about learning. While physics was not a subject that I was initially very interested in, I enjoyed how my professor organized his lectures and made me think. I was impressed by how thoughtful he was about educating his students and how he implemented his educational beliefs in his class.

Much to my great disappointment, I did very poorly on the mid-term examination and barely got a C-minus.[1] I thought I understood the material much better than that grade reflected. All I could think of was how the class was going to bring down my GPA and hurt my chances of getting into medical school; I was demoralized. When it was time to take the final examination in the course, I was very anxious about how well I would do, given my poor performance in the mid-term exam.

My professor had briefed us on the final test: He would start with the most straightforward questions, and each subsequent question would be harder to answer. The final question would be so difficult he considered it to be an "extra credit" bonus question. This question wouldn't count against you if you didn't answer it correctly, but it could help boost your grade if you got it right.

I will always remember nervously sitting down and opening up the test booklet. I looked over the first, "easiest" problem. After reading it, my mind drew a complete blank. Nothing. That had never happened to me before in my life. Surprised, I calmly thought I would just move to the next question and come back to the first question later. Much to my horror, I looked at the following question and, again, I couldn't think of how to answer the question. I then quickly moved on to the next question and then the next one, only to face the same result. I was near the end of the test booklet and had not been able to answer a single question. I started to panic.

I decided I had better stand up and go to the bathroom. Not that I needed to relieve myself; I just needed to leave the examination hall and pull myself together. Sitting in the bathroom stall, I took some deep breaths and told myself that I could do it. I said to myself that I understood the material and could finish the test.

I finally decided to walk back into the test hall with only half of the time remaining. The only question I hadn't seen yet was the difficult extra credit question. I decided to work on that one next. Suddenly, it all made

---

[1] At the time, no one got lower than a "C-minus" on a course at Stanford. Instead, they usually dropped out of the course before it ended. In other words, I did very poorly on that exam.

sense to me. The portion of my brain that held my physics knowledge finally decided to switch on. As I answered that question, I realized that the answer I wrote down had to be correct. Now confident, I flipped back the pages of the test, quickly solving the first problem that had initially stumped me so completely. I finished the entire examination early with plenty of time left.

The next week, when I went to look for my grade (in those days, our grades were posted outside of the classroom; we were identified not by our names but our student numbers to provide some confidentiality) for the exam and course, I discovered I had achieved the second highest score in the class on the examination, but my extra credit question had boosted my score to the very top. I ended with an A-minus in the overall course, making me extraordinarily happy given my poor first mid-term exam score.

Never again did I do as well on any single examination in college as I did on that particular physics test. But this personal experience left a huge impression on me. I understood in a genuine way how my emotions and attitudes could impact on my academic performance. I never underestimated its power after that. As a result, in subsequent examinations, I did not try to cram the last bit of information into my head right before heading into the examination room. Instead, I would go to bed on time the night before, and wake up early to calm myself, gain focus on my thoughts, and visualize my success on the examination.

Email Your Advice Activity
(Approximate Duration: 10 minutes or Longer)

Imagine that your younger brother (or sister or friend) is struggling in his math class in school. He is getting discouraged and beginning to feel that he doesn't belong in his school; he sees his classmates as so different from him and is lonely. He writes you an email asking for your advice. What would you say in your reply to him?

Aim: Reflect further regarding the impact of feelings on academic performance.

Instructions: Write a reply email (at least 1–2 paragraphs) to him with your best advice, including any ideas/strategies you have developed from reading this book.

Conclusion

Growth mindset and stereotype threat

"One can choose to go back toward safety or forward toward growth. Growth must be chosen again and again; fear must be overcome again and again."

— Abraham Maslow —

Educational research backs the powerful influences exemplified by my personal story. One of the most important findings is that those who attribute their academic success to a natural but unchangeable or "fixed" intelligence will not do as well academically as those who believe that their intelligence can "grow." These latter individuals believe any setbacks that they experience are due to time-limited reasons and will improve over time. This perspective is commonly known as the "growth mindset," and it shapes your ability to reach your fullest potential in life (Dweck, 2017). If you have chosen to read this book to the end, you have a growth mindset!

Pairing a growth mindset with a crystal-clear vision of the goals that you believe to be worth pursuing, effective learning strategies, and the rest of the Metacognitive Cycle is critical for your strategic learning plan. A growth mindset provides comfort, suggesting that failure is only temporary and not the end; it is a natural part of a longer journey to success. It encourages you to seek new challenges as an excellent opportunity to learn more, rather than as a risk to avoid. It reminds you to persevere with your efforts and keep striving to reach even higher standards. The attitude that stems from a growth mindset serves as a powerful inspiration for your ability to learn better.

As I explained earlier, a critical difference with the best learners is what they learn from the inevitable setbacks that occur. If things don't work out as expected, the best learners use something like the Holistic Learning Framework to figure out where the problem might be and try another approach to studying. They don't give up; they don't decide they aren't cut out to learn or that they don't belong to the group of people that can learn more quickly than them. They just say to themselves, "I haven't figured out how to best learn it yet."

Along with your belief that you can improve your performance, there is evidence that the opposite is also true: Your mind can significantly limit your performance depending on your negative beliefs in yourself. The research on how negative stereotypes held by others can influence your performance is known as "stereotype threat" (Steele & Aronson, 1995). We tend to "live up or down" to the stereotyped images that others have about us, and as a result, we start to believe these stereotypes apply to ourselves as well.

This impact occurs even on a subconscious level. For example, a stereotype held by some is that women are not naturally good at mathematics and science. Studies reveal that when told the exam has no gender bias right before taking an examination, these women students will do better (Good, Aronson, & Harder, 2008; Spencer, Steele, & Quinn, 1999). Although some still debate the validity of studies in this research area, most agree that many factors other than intelligence seem to play significant roles in academic performance (Eschenbach *et al.*, 2014).

Similarly, I see my students at NUS suffering from some pretty harsh negative self-talk. When I ask them what keeps them from reaching their academic goals, the most common reason I hear is that they are "too lazy" to do well. Well, I know if they were able to gain admission to Singapore's flagship public university, they must have had worked very hard and are not lazy. Perhaps they choose to be hard on themselves as a way to motivate themselves to perform better. Unfortunately, negative self-talk can lead to demotivation and impaired performance too.

Now take another look at the "Email your advice" activity that you did, and re-read what you wrote. Is there any advice there that you could use for yourself?

Whether it is a lack of self-confidence, stereotype threat or a having a fixed mindset, I suggest that you learn more about the psychology that enhances or detracts from performance. This chapter can only provide a broad introduction to these influences on learning. Besides the book already referenced above, *Mindsets by Carol Dweck*, other good places to learn more about this subject include books written by well-known academics: *Grit* by Angela Duckworth and *Whistling Vivaldi* by Claude Steele. (Duckworth, 2016; Steele, 2011) The references to the literature that I have included in this book would also be a great way to learn more about this aspect of learning.

Your strategic learning approach

Over the years, I have learned about and now firmly believe in the importance of leading a balanced life with family and friends while carrying out other pursuits besides academics. I used to think that the only way you can learn more is by finding or creating more time to study and learn. I've rarely heard people complain they have so much extra time that they don't know what to do with it. And I'm still waiting to find anyone who knows how to create another hour in the day. I believe that time is the most valuable asset that we have; if there were more time, there would undoubtedly be more for us to learn, more exercise, more fun with friends and family, etc. Becoming more efficient with your learning should be everyone's goal. As I insist to my students, "take your time and study hard but don't waste your time!"

To me, the most successful (and happiest) students are neither the hardest workers nor the most intelligent. Instead, the most successful students are the ones who are the most strategic. They set goals that are meaningful to them, rather than for someone else or what they think society wants from them. Although they often do, they might not necessarily get the best grades; instead, they get the grades that are most consistent with their personal goals. Most importantly, they maximize their efficiency, given the time they have committed to studying. As a result, they achieve their best, given their personal goals and abilities. They are in control of their success, in whatever way they choose to define it.

I hope that after reading this book, you now realize that there are more factors that impact your ability to learn than you first thought. And the best way to improve your learning is by taking a strategic, holistic approach.

Final Thoughts on the Power of Thoughts

Apply what you have learned from this book, and you will not regret the effort involved. No doubt, not everything covered in this book pertains to you, and certain parts will help you more than others. It is now up to you to figure out how to best implement a learning plan that fits you. Keep celebrating your small wins, forgive yourself for your failures and keep adjusting things until they are "just right."

I especially encourage you to hold on to whatever great aspirational goals you have in life. My other wish for you is to continue to choose change for yourself, rather than staying stuck in the same place, doing the same things because of fear. Over our lives, we tend to regret the times when we didn't do something more than the times when we tried to do something but failed. You now have a strategic approach that will help you formulate the changes and steps necessary to achieve your life-long learning success.

"Live as if you were to die tomorrow. Learn as if you were to live forever."
— Mahatma Gandhi —

If any part of this book has made a difference for you, I would enjoy hearing about it from you. I would learn a great deal from your experiences and comments. I welcome you to send me a note: strategiclearn.kamei@gmail.com

Best of luck with your life-long learning journey.

References

Duckworth, A. (2016). *Grit: The Power of Passion and Perseverance.* Scribner: New York.

Dweck, C. (2017). *Mindset-Updated Edition: Changing the Way You Think to Fulfil Your Potential.* Hachette: UK.

Eschenbach, E. A., Virnoche, M., Cashman, E. M., Lord, S. M., & Camacho, M. M. (2014). *Proven practices that can reduce stereotype threat in engineering education: A literature review.* Paper presented at the 2014 IEEE Frontiers in Education Conference (FIE) Proceedings.

Good, C., Aronson, J., & Harder, J. A. (2008). Problems in the pipeline: Stereotype threat and women's achievement in high-level math courses. *Journal of Applied Developmental Psychology,* **29**(1), 17–28.

Spencer, S. J., Steele, C. M., & Quinn, D. M. (1999). Stereotype threat and women's math performance. *Journal of Experimental Social Psychology,* **35**(1), 4–28.

Steele, C. M. (2011). *Whistling Vivaldi: How Stereotypes Affect Us and What We Can Do.* W. W. Norton & Company: New York.

Steele, C. M., & Aronson, J. (1995). Stereotype threat and the intellectual test performance of African Americans. *Journal of Personality and Social Psychology,* **69**(5), 797.

Yeager, D. S., & Walton, G. M. (2011). Social-psychological interventions in education: They're not magic. *Review of Educational Research,* **81**(2), 267–301.

Appendices

Appendix A

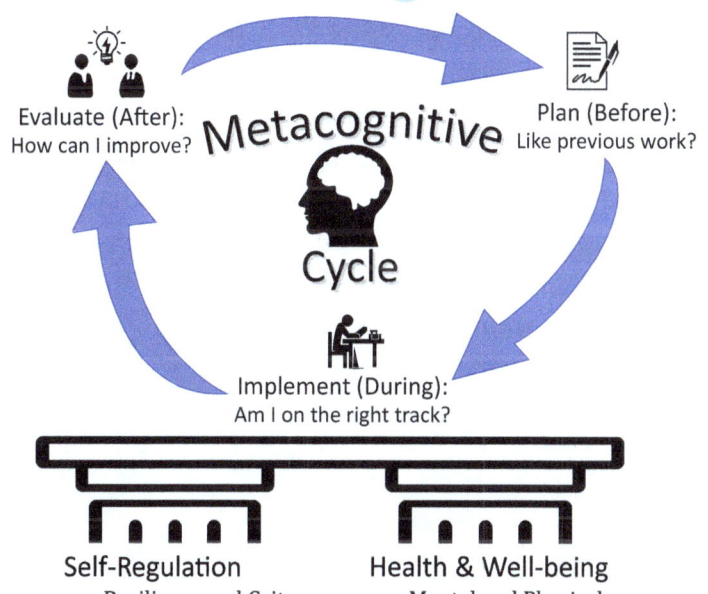

Appendices

Although this figure is already included in several places in the book, I place another copy here as a place where you can keep track of the ideas that make the most sense for you to implement into your learning plan. I suggest that you write a word or two about the strategies you most wish to try out next to the relevant parts of the framework. You might find it easier to keep track of these ideas by including the appropriate page numbers in your note too.

Appendix B

Mind maps are a visual representation of how different concepts, items, and tasks relate to a central concept or subject. It uses a branching hierarchical structure to allow for more complex, non-linear information to be neatly organized, stored and reviewed. Some mind maps will use different lines, colors or images to provide additional organization or information. Mind maps can be used to take lecture notes or review previously learned topics. I especially like them because you are not constrained by putting items on your mind map in any particular order; as a result it can be a helpful technique to brainstorm on new ideas.

Mind maps are easily created using paper and pencil. There are also several free and commercial software programs available to help create larger mind maps or easily re-organize and edit the branches. Some mind maps can get quite elaborate and large, but there is not one "correct" method of doing it. Just find what works best for you!

Appendices

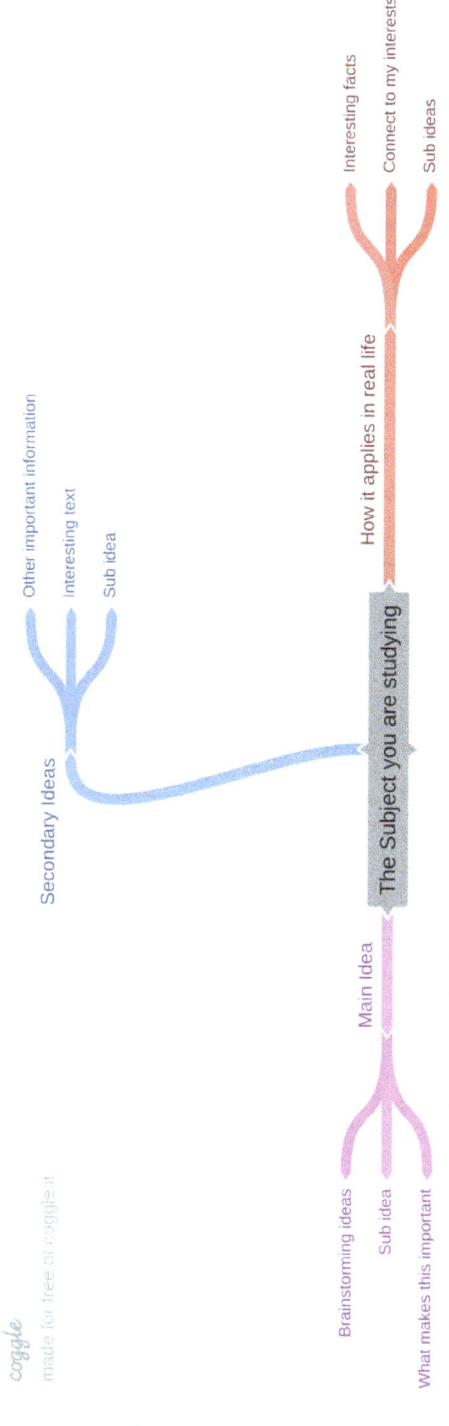

Example of a mind map created using Coggle (which has a free plan). Links to this and other mind map programs at www.strategiclearn.org under "Resources\Other links."

Appendix C

Having a Team Charter is a good practice for any study group. It sets the tone for the team, which importantly includes how members can openly communicate with each other. It helps deal at the very beginning with the different expectations that each member has of the team. It is much easier to deal with these differences at the start than after members have worked together for some time and then discover they have different ideas about their group.

I've included a copy of the team charter similar to the one we use at Duke-NUS Medical School. Since we have a curriculum centered around teamwork (it is a vital skill in medical practice!), we use this charter in a formal manner and have all members sign on it. However, feel free to use this charter only as a guide directing your initial group conversation. You can download a copy of this Team Charter Template from the www.strategiclearn.org website (Resources\Downloadables). There are different team charters for study groups available on the internet, so search around if you would prefer something slightly different.

Study team charter

PURPOSE (VISION): WRITE A FEW SENTENCES DESCRIBING WHY YOU EXIST AS A TEAM AND WHAT YOU INTEND TO ACHIEVE TOGETHER.

OPERATING PRINCIPLES: WHAT ARE THE SPECIFIC BEHAVIORS AND OPERATING PRINCIPLES YOU AGREE TO IN ORDER TO ACHIEVE THE RESULTS YOU DESIRE AS INDIVIDUALS AND AS A TEAM?

Communication (What basic communication guidelines will you agree to? How will you approach giving and receiving feedback?)

Leadership (What leadership/administration does the team need? For instance, setting meeting times, agenda, other types of communication How will leadership be determined/shared?)

Coordination (How will you share responsibility and accountability for team results and ensure everyone is aligned?)

COMMUNITY: WHAT TEAM CULTURE, NETWORKS AND RELATIONSHIPS BEYOND THE TEAM DO YOU WANT TO CREATE? HOW WILL YOU SUPPORT ONE ANOTHER IN MAINTAINING FOCUS AND BALANCE – AS INDIVIDUALS AND AS A TEAM?

Collaboration (How will you share different ideas and ensure that everyone is contributing and being listened to? How will you evaluate ideas and make decisions?)

Knowing the Team (How will you discover and fully utilize the diverse personalities, strengths, knowledge, skills and talents on your team?)

Conflict (How will you ensure that team members feel free to express their point of view? How will you resolve differences of opinion, enforce operating principles, and recognize cultural and personal preferences?)

Appendix D

A learning plan can be developed using many different formats, and this can be done using an informal or formal process. The format doesn't matter as long as it is useful to you. Any plan should remind you of your important aspirational goals and more specific SMART goals. Just writing down your aspirational and SMART goals makes it more likely you will work towards them and achieve them! Most students create a learning plan that covers their upcoming semester only. Your aspirational goals generally won't change very frequently, but your SMART goals should change more often. Your strategic learning plan document should not ever be considered finished, but instead a work in progress that changes over time.

For those of you looking for more guidance on how to best document your learning plan, I have included below a step by step example which includes goal setting, completing the Metacognitive Cycle, considering your learning foundations of Self-Regulation and Health & Wellbeing. This is the format that we use to guide students taking our NUS course. There is also an accompanied calendar useful for strategizing how you will accomplish your plan. I suggest you start small and try not to be overly ambitious with this plan at the start. Don't be too complete with your SMART goals, otherwise you can end up with thousands of goals. Perhaps one or two high priority SMART goals is all you need to start. Don't forget to consider aspects you think will keep you from accomplishing your goals as well.

Since the plan should evolve over time, the sample strategic working document below has three versions, each representing a different moment in time during the Metacognitive Cycle. If you feel this format will be of help, you can download a blank template from my website (www.strategiclearn.org under "Resources\Downloadables").

Consider reviewing your learning plan with a friend, family member or faculty advisor that you trust. They can help keep you motivated to stay on your plan or provide advice for you to adjust the plan appropriately.

Example Strategic Learning Plan

Step 1: Setting your goals

Determine your Aspirational Goals (What are your lifetime ambitions? What would you like to achieve at the end of this year (or longer time frame)?):

Examples:

1. Get on the Dean's List for academic achievement
2. Improve my health and finish a triathlon sometime during this year
3. Get into medical school and become a doctor

Determine a set of SMART Goals: (Are they **S**pecific, **M**easureable, **A**chieveable, **R**elevant, **T**ime-based?); these should directly address one or more of your aspirational goals.

Examples:

1. Implement spaced learning during my Physics study rather than cram at the last minute for this upcoming semester
2. Organize a study group to help me better understand what is the most important issues to concentrate my learning for my History Class
3. Improve my self-motivation: research why my classes that I'm taking this semester are relevant to my aspirational goals
4. Go to the gym to work out on a treadmill for 1 hour 3 times/week
5. Minimize distractions and stay off my phone when I study History to improve my focus during this upcoming semester

Step 2: Take a few of your SMART goals above and place in the first column of the Learning Plan: Strategic Working Document. Add to the "Plan" column your ideas and learning strategies you want to use to accomplish these SMART Goals. Consider keeping your plan in your learning calendar as well, it will make it easier to follow. I suggest this step be done at the beginning of each semester.

Learning Plan: Strategic Working Document (Planning Phase)

Updated: 19 August 2020

Holistic Learning Framework	Metacognitive Cycle		
SMART Goals	Plan	Implement	Evaluate
Learning Strategies			
1. Implement spaced learning in my Physics course	Schedule in my calendar, the date/time and the chapters I will study, with the last study session within 24 hours of the final examination.		
2. Organize a History Study Group	Ask 3 others to join me in a study group. We can discuss the main points covered that week. I will treat myself to my favorite espresso after attending each session.		

Appendices

(*Continued*)

Holistic Learning Framework SMART Goals	Metacognitive Cycle		
	Plan	Implement	Evaluate

Self-Regulation

3. Improve my self-motivation by increasing my internal motivation to learn

   Plan: Research why the material covered in the class is important for my future career. I will do a Google search for 1 hr during the first week of class and discuss my findings with my professor.

Health & Wellbeing

4. Improve my general health with the aspirational goal of completing a triathlon

   Plan: I won't go to the gym if I don't commit to it ahead of time and put it in my schedule.

5. Improve my focus when I study history

   Plan: Keep my phone in my backpack during my history study time so I'm not tempted to use it.

169

Appendices

Step 3: Sometime during the semester, keep notes on how your plan is going in the Implement Column. You don't need to make any major changes in your plan at this point in time.

Learning Plan: Strategic Working Document (Implement Phase)

Last updated: 19 October 2020

Holistic Learning Framework Goals	Metacognitive Cycle		
	Plan	Implement	Evaluate
Learning Strategies			
Implement spaced learning in my Physics course	Schedule the date/time and the chapters I will study, with the last study session within 24 hours of the final examination.	I found that I wasn't able to finish what I wanted to study each session and had to take more time. I mostly read/re-read the materials.	
Organize a History Study Group	Ask 3 others to join me in a study group. We can discuss the main points covered that week. I will treat myself to my favorite espresso before attending each session.	It was easy to find classmates interested in forming a study group, but hard to find a time to meet.	

Holistic Learning Framework Goals	Metacognitive Cycle		
	(Continued)		
	Plan	Implement	Evaluate
Self-Regulation			
Improve my self-motivation by increasing my internal motivation to learn.	Research why the material covered in the class is important for my future career. I will do a Google search for 1 hr during the first week of class and discuss my findings with my professor.	I was motivated to understand the topic better but it was hard to work up courage to meet my professor for a consultation.	
Health & Wellbeing			
Improve my general health with the aspirational goal of completing a triathlon.	I won't go to the gym if I don't commit to it ahead of time and put it in my schedule.	I made it to 75% of my scheduled sessions, at times some things just came up and I couldn't go.	
Improve my focus when I study History.	Keep my phone in my backpack during my History study time so I'm not tempted to use it.	I was able to do this, but my mom got mad when I didn't answer the phone right away. Nevertheless, I felt better prepared for my History class.	

Step 4: At a pre-determined time (usually after the semester is complete), you should evaluate your goals, plan and implementation (using the "3 Rs" Review, Reflect and Revise). Then start again with a new strategic working document!

Learning Plan: Strategic Working Document (Evaluate Phase)

Last updated: 5 January 2021

Holistic Learning Framework Goals	Metacognitive Cycle		
	Plan	Implement	Evaluate
Learning Strategies			
Implement spaced learning in my Physics course	Schedule the date/time and the chapters I will study, with the last study session within 24 hours of the final examination.	I found that I wasn't able to finish what I wanted to study each session and had to take more time. I mostly read/re-read the materials.	I thought I could do better in this course. Next semester, I will plan more time to study this and practice more test questions I found on the internet.
Organize a History Study Group	Ask 3 others to join me in a study group. We can discuss the main points covered that week. I will treat myself to my favorite espresso before attending each session.	It was easy to find classmates interested in forming a study group, but hard to find a time to meet.	The study group really helped me when we were able to meet. I really looked forward to it, especially because I had my coffee during the meeting. Next time I will choose people who also prioritize this study strategy.

(Continued)

Holistic Learning Framework Goals	Metacognitive Cycle		
	Plan	Implement	Evaluate
Self-Regulation			
Improve my self-motivation by increasing my internal motivation to learn.	Research why the material covered in the class is important for my future career. I will do a Google search for 1 hr during the first week of class and discuss my findings with my professor.	I was motivated to understand the topic better but it was hard to work up the courage to meet my professor for a consultation.	I won't beat myself up for not meeting with my prof, but start by aiming to ask a question at the end of class.
Health & Wellbeing			
Improve my general health with the aspirational goal of completing a triathlon	I won't go to the gym if I don't commit to it ahead of time and put it in my schedule.	I made it to 75% of my scheduled sessions, at times some things just came up and I couldn't go.	I went to a lot of social activities that weren't that important to me, instead of working out. I will also try to plan alternative times to work out in case I have to miss one of my sessions.

(Continued)

(Continued)

Holistic Learning Framework Goals	Metacognitive Cycle		
	Plan	Implement	Evaluate
Improve my focus when I study History	Keep my phone in my backpack during my History study time so I'm not tempted to use it.	I was able to do this, but my mom got mad when I didn't answer the phone right away. Nevertheless, I felt better prepared for my History class.	My History grade improved. I'll schedule more breaks during my study period. I need to inform my family when I won't be available by phone.

Appendices

My Sample Learning Plan Calendar: Dec 2020

Sun	Mon	Tue	Wed	Thu	Fri	Sat
			1 Physics Class (8-11am); Physics Practice Test (8-11pm)	**2** Workout (8:30-10am); History Study Grp (10-12am); History Class (2-4pm)	**3** Physics Class (8-11am); Physics Study Grp (3-4pm); Hanging w/ Friends (6-11pm)	**4** Hanging w/ Friends (6-12pm)
5 Workout (9-10:30am)	**6** Physics Class (8-11am); Physics Consultation (3-4pm); Pre-Class History preparation (4-5pm); Physics Review Chapts 1-2 (7-10pm)	**7** History Class (2-4pm); Physics Homework (4-6pm); Workout (7-8:30pm)	**8** Physics Class (8-11am); Physics Practice Test (8-11pm)	**9** Workout (8:30-10am); History Study Grp (10-12am); History Class (2-4pm); Physics Homework (4-6pm)	**10** Physics Class (8-11am); Physics Study Grp (3-4pm); Hanging w/ Friends (6-11pm)	**11** Hanging w/ Friends (6-12pm)
12 Workout (9-10:30am)	**13** Physics Class (8-11am); Pre-Class History preparation (4-5pm); Physics Review Chapts 3-4 (7-10pm)	**14** History Class (2-4pm); Physics Homework (4-6pm); Workout (7-8:30pm)	**15** Physics Class (8-11am); Physics Practice Test (8-11pm)	**16** Workout (8:30-10am); History Study Grp (10-12am); History Class (2-4pm); Physics Homework (4-6pm)	**17** Physics Class (8-11am); Physics Study Grp (3-4pm); Hanging w/ Friends (6-11pm)	**18** Hanging w/ Friends (6-12pm)

Reading/Revision Week

Sun	Mon	Tue	Wed	Thu	Fri	Sat
19 Workout (9-10:30am)	**20** Physics Review Chapts 5-6 (9-12am)	**21** Physics Review Chapts 7-8 (9-12am); Workout (7-8:30pm)	**22** Physics Review Chapts 9-10 (9-12am); Physics Practice Test (8-11pm)	**23** Workout (8:30-10am); History Study Grp (10-12am); Physics Review Chapts 11-12 (9-12am)	**24** Physics Study Grp (3-4pm); Hanging w/ Friends (6-12pm)	**25** Hanging w/ Friends (6-12pm)
26 Workout (9-10:30am)	**27**	**28** Workout (7-8:30pm)				

Examination Week

Sun	Mon	Tue	Wed	Thu	Fri	Sat
29 History Final Exam (2-4pm)	**30** Workout (8:30-10am); Physics Final Review (6-11pm); Early Sleep Time (11PM)	**31** Physics Final Exam (8-11)				

Appendix E

For the teachers reading this book who are looking to improve their own learning and help guide their students on how to learn better, I'm pleased that you are interested in being guided by the best scientific evidence we have. There continues to be considerable research on how people learn best and it is my hope and expectation that many aspects of this book become outdated as we learn more about learning.

It is obvious that helping your students become better learners as covered in this book is only one way to influence their academic achievements. How you teach, the curriculum chosen and the teaching strategy that is used for your students, does make a difference. Those interested in understanding more about what works for learning and understanding how well it works can find some incredible free resources of information. I recommend starting with the "What Works Clearinghouse" website sponsored by the United States Department of Education. This site contains critical reviews of research on educational programs, practices and policies intending to help make the information learned from these studies more available to educators.

The other comprehensive resource is Prof John Hattie's "Visible Learning: A Synthesis of Over 800 Meta-analyses Relating to Achievement." This remarkable book is a "review of educational research reviews." This book presents a particular type of scientific literature on education known as "meta-analyses," which critically analyzes research papers covering the same topic and combines them in a way to increase the credibility of any conclusions made. Therefore, he estimates his book includes data from over 50,000 individual studies!

Bibliography

Alter, A. L. (2013). The benefits of cognitive disfluency. *Current Directions in Psychological Science*, **22**(6), 437–442.

Ang, J. (2020). Singapore IB students make up half of world's perfect scorers. *Straits Times,* Jan 4. Retrieved from https://www.straitstimes.com/singapore/education/spore-ib-students-make-up-half-of-worlds-perfect-scorers.

Ariga, A., & Lleras, A. (2011). Brief and rare mental "breaks" keep you focused: Deactivation and reactivation of task goals preempt vigilance decrements. *Cognition*, **118**(3), 439–443.

Avila, C., Furnham, A., & McClelland, A. (2012). The influence of distracting familiar vocal music on cognitive performance of introverts and extraverts. *Psychology of Music*, **40**(1), 84–93.

Ball, K., Berch, D. B., Helmers, K. F., Jobe, J. B., Leveck, M. D., Marsiske, M., & Tennstedt, S. L. (2002). Effects of cognitive training interventions with older adults: A randomized controlled trial. *Jama*, **288**(18), 2271–2281.

Becker, M. W., Alzahabi, R., & Hopwood, C. J. (2013). Media multitasking is associated with symptoms of depression and social anxiety. *Cyberpsychology, Behavior, and Social Networking*, **16**(2), 132–135.

Bjork, E. L., & Bjork, R. A. (2011). Making things hard on yourself, but in a good way: Creating desirable difficulties to enhance learning. In *Psychology and the Real World: Essays Illustrating Fundamental Contributions to Society,* M. A. Gernsbacher, R. W. Pew, L. M. Hough, J. R. Pomerantz (eds.), 59–68, Worth Publishers: New York.

Cepeda, N. J., Pashler, H., Vul, E., Wixted, J. T., & Rohrer, D. (2006). Distributed practice in verbal recall tasks: A review and quantitative synthesis. *Psychological Bulletin*, **132**(3), 354.

Chu, S., & Downes, J. J. (2002). Proust nose best: Odors are better cues of autobiographical memory. *Memory & Cognition*, **30**(4), 511–518.

Chua, A. (2011). *Battle Hymn of the Tiger Mother.* Bloomsbury Publishing: London.

Cialdini, R. (2016). *Pre-suasion: A Revolutionary Way to Influence and Persuade.* Simon and Schuster: New York.

Cowan, N. (2008). What are the differences between long-term, short-term, and working memory? *Progress in Brain Research*, **169**, 323–338.

Cuevas, J. (2015). Is learning styles-based instruction effective? A comprehensive analysis of recent research on learning styles. *Theory and Research in Education*, **13**(3), 308–333.

Dawson, D. & Reid, K. (1997). Fatigue, alcohol and performance impairment. *Nature*, **388**(6639), 235–235.

Deslauriers, L., McCarty, L. S., Miller, K., Callaghan, K., & Kestin, G. (2019). Measuring actual learning versus feeling of learning in response to being actively engaged in the classroom. *Proceedings of the National Academy of Sciences*, **116**(39), 19251–19257.

Diemand-Yauman, C., Oppenheimer, D. M., & Vaughan, E. B. (2011). Fortune favors the: Effects of disfluency on educational outcomes. *Cognition*, **118**(1), 114–118.

Duckworth, A. (2016). *Grit: The Power of Passion and Perseverance.* Scribner: New York.

Dweck, C. (2017). *Mindset-Updated Edition: Changing the Way You Think to Fulfil Your Potential.* Hachette: UK.

Ebbinghaus, H. (1913). *Memory* (H. A. Ruger & C. E. Bussenius, trans.). Teachers College: New York, 39.(Original work published 1885.)

Elhussein, G., Leopold, A., & Zahidi, S. (2020). Schools of the Future: Defining New Models of Education for the Fourth Industrial Revolution. Future Skills Centre, Canada. Retrieved from https://fsc-ccf.ca/references/schools-of-the-future-defining-new-models-of-education-for-the-fourth-industrial-revolution/.

Ericsson, K. A., & Harwell, K. W. (2019). Deliberate practice and proposed limits on the effects of practice on the acquisition of expert performance: Why the original definition matters and recommendations for future research. *Frontiers in Psychology*, **10**(2396), doi:10.3389/fpsyg.2019.02396.

Ertmer, P. A., & Newby, T. J. (1996). The expert learner: Strategic, self-regulated, and reflective. *Instructional Science*, **24**(1), 1–24.

Eschenbach, E. A., Virnoche, M., Cashman, E. M., Lord, S. M., & Camacho, M. M. (2014). *Proven practices that can reduce stereotype threat in engineering education: A literature review.* Paper presented at the 2014 IEEE Frontiers in Education Conference (FIE) Proceedings.

Bibliography

Foer, J. (2012). *Moonwalking with Einstein: The Art and Science of Remembering Everything*. Penguin: New York.

Gladwell, M. (2008). *Outliers: The Story of Success*. Little, Brown: New York.

Godden, D. R., & Baddeley, A. D. (1975). Context dependent memory in two natural environments: On land and underwater. *British Journal of Psychology*, **66**(3), 325–331.

Good, C., Aronson, J., & Harder, J. A. (2008). Problems in the pipeline: Stereotype threat and women's achievement in high-level math courses. *Journal of Applied Developmental Psychology*, **29**(1), 17–28.

Hall, K. G., Domingues, D. A., & Cavazos, R. (1994). Contextual interference effects with skilled baseball players. *Perceptual and Motor Skills*, **78**(3), 835–841.

Harari, Y. N. (2014). *Sapiens: A Brief History of Humankind*. Random House: UK.

Haraszti, R. Á., Ella, K., Gyöngyösi, N., Roenneberg, T., & Káldi, K. (2014). Social jetlag negatively correlates with academic performance in undergraduates. *Chronobiology International*, **31**(5), 603–612.

Hattie, J. A. C. (2009). *Visible Learning: A Synthesis of Over 800 Meta — Analyses Relating to Achievement*. Routledge: London.

Hessler, M., et al. (2018). Availability of cookies during an academic course session affects evaluation of teaching. *Medical Education*, **52**(10), 1064–1072.

Hillman, C. H., Erickson, K. I., & Kramer, A. F. (2008). Be smart, exercise your heart: Exercise effects on brain and cognition. *Nature Reviews Neuroscience*, **9**(1), 58–65.

Huang, S.-C., & Aaker, J. (2019). It's the journey, not the destination: How metaphor drives growth after goal attainment. *Journal of Personality and Social Psychology*, **117**(4), 697–720.

Hulleman, C. S., & Harackiewicz, J. M. (2009). Promoting interest and performance in high school science classes. *Science*, **326**(5958), 1410–1412.

Karpicke, J. D., & Bauernschmidt, A. (2011). Spaced retrieval: absolute spacing enhances learning regardless of relative spacing. *Journal of Experimental Psychology: Learning, Memory, and Cognition*, **37**(5), 1250.

Killingsworth, M. A., & Gilbert, D. T. (2010). A wandering mind is an unhappy mind. *Science*, **330**(6006), 932–932.

Kornell, N., & Bjork, R. A. (2008). Learning concepts and categories: Is spacing the "enemy of induction"? *Psychological Science*, **19**(5), 585–592.

Kraschnewski, J., Boan, J., Esposito, J., Sherwood, N. E., Lehman, E. B., Kephart, D. K., & Sciamanna, C. (2010). Long-term weight loss maintenance in the United States. *International Journal of Obesity*, **34**(11), 1644–1654.

Krathwohl, D. R., & Anderson, L. W. (2009). *A Taxonomy for Learning, Teaching, and Assessing: A Revision of Bloom's Taxonomy of Educational Objectives.* Longman: New York.

Lawlor, K. B. (2012). *Smart goals: How the application of smart goals can contribute to achievement of student learning outcomes.* Paper presented at the Developments in Business Simulation and Experiential Learning: Proceedings of the Annual ABSEL Conference.

Lehmann, J. A., & Seufert, T. (2017). The influence of background music on learning in the light of different theoretical perspectives and the role of working memory capacity. *Frontiers in Psychology*, **8**, 1902.

Li, P., Legault, J., & Litcofsky, K. A. (2014). Neuroplasticity as a function of second language learning: anatomical changes in the human brain. *Cortex*, **58**, 301–324.

Maddox, G. B. (2016). Understanding the underlying mechanism of the spacing effect in verbal learning: A case for encoding variability and study-phase retrieval. *Journal of Cognitive Psychology*, **28**(6), 684–706.

Murre, J. M., & Dros, J. (2015). Replication and analysis of Ebbinghaus' forgetting curve. *PloS one*, **10**(7), https://doi.org/10.1371/journal.pone.0120644.

Oettingen, G., Mayer, D., & Brinkmann, B. (2010). Mental contrasting of future and reality. *Journal of Personnel Psychology*, **9**(3), 138–144.

Pink, D. H. (2011). *Drive: The Surprising Truth About What Motivates Us.* Penguin: London.

Quigley, A., Muijs, D., & Stringer, E. (2018). Metacognition and self-regulated learning: Guidance report. Education Endowment Foundation: UK.

Ramsburg, J. T., & Youmans, R. J. (2014). Meditation in the higher-education classroom: Meditation training improves student knowledge retention during lectures. *Mindfulness*, **5**(4), 431–441.

Rohrer, D. (2012). Interleaving helps students distinguish among similar concepts. *Educational Psychology Review*, **24**(3), 355–367.

Rosen, L. D., Carrier, L. M., & Cheever, N. A. (2013). Facebook and texting made me do it: Media-induced task-switching while studying. *Computers in Human Behavior*, **29**(3), 948–958.

Sanbonmatsu, D. M., Strayer, D. L., Medeiros-Ward, N., & Watson, J. M. (2013). Who multi-tasks and why? Multi-tasking ability, perceived multi-tasking ability, impulsivity, and sensation seeking. *PloS one*, **8**(1), e54402.

Schleicher, A. (2019). PISA 2018: Insights and Interpretations. *OECD Publishing*.

Seli, P., Beaty, R. E., Cheyne, J. A., Smilek, D., Oakman, J., & Schacter, D. L. (2018). How pervasive is mind wandering, really? *Consciousness and Cognition*, **66**, 74–78.

Bibliography

Simon, D. A., & Bjork, R. A. (2001). Metacognition in motor learning. *Journal of Experimental Psychology: Learning, Memory, and Cognition*, **27**(4), 907.

Sirois, F., & Pychyl, T. (2013). Procrastination and the priority of short term mood regulation: Consequences for future self. *Social and Personality Psychology Compass*, **7**(2), 115–127.

Spencer, S. J., Steele, C. M., & Quinn, D. M. (1999). Stereotype threat and women's math performance. *Journal of Experimental Social Psychology*, **35**(1), 4–28.

Steele, C. M. (2011). *Whistling Vivaldi: How Stereotypes Affect Us and What We Can Do.* W. W. Norton & Company: New York.

Steele, C. M., & Aronson, J. (1995). Stereotype threat and the intellectual test performance of African Americans. *Journal of Personality and Social Psychology*, **69**(5), 797.

Steinborn, M. B. & Huestegge, L. (2016). A walk down the lane gives wings to your brain. Restorative benefits of rest breaks on cognition and self control. *Applied Cognitive Psychology*, **30**(5), 795–805.

Tanner, K. D. (2012). Promoting student metacognition. *CBE — Life Sciences Education*, **11**(2), 113–120.

Tharp, T. (2008). *The Creative Habit,* Simon and Schuster: New York.

Tulving, E., & Thomson, D. M. (1973). Encoding specificity and retrieval processes in episodic memory. *Psychological Review*, **80**(5), 352.

Willingham, D. T. (2009). *Why Don't Students Like School?: A Cognitive Scientist Answers Questions About How The Mind Works And What It Means For The Classroom.* John Wiley & Sons: New Jersey.

Xie, L., Kang, H., Xu, Q., Chen, M. J., Liao, Y., Thiyagarajan, M., & Iliff, J. J. (2013). Sleep drives metabolite clearance from the adult brain. *Science*, **342**(6156), 373–377.

Yeager, D. S., & Walton, G. M. (2011). Social-psychological interventions in education: They're not magic. *Review of Educational Research*, **81**(2), 267–301.

Zaharna, M., & Guilleminault, C. (2010). Sleep, noise and health. *Noise and Health*, **12**(47), 64.

Zimmerman, B. J. (2002). Becoming a self-regulated learner: An overview. *Theory into Practice*, **41**(2), 64–70.

Some Additional Information and Resources

After finishing my National University of Singapore "Learning to Learn Better" course (and sometimes even after graduating from NUS), several of my students continue to ask me new questions they have about learning. They are often curious about an aspect that I didn't have enough time to cover in class, or they discovered on their own. In addition, I found many other students outside of NUS were interested in learning more about learning too. As a result, I created a public website (www.strategiclearn.org) to serve as a learning community "gathering site" where people could exchange new study ideas, pose questions, and could read the latest information about learning. The site has a blog written by students and faculty covering various ways to learn better, all referenced with the most important academic papers for those interested in reading further. The website also has a Forum where visitors can submit comments or questions to our community.

Readers of this book will recognize this site as a place where our online activities reside and where they can download examples of learning tools and plans. There are also links to some other interesting websites with information or tools that might help learners. We have also placed a few short videos we use in our NUS class that complements our in-class teaching or

Some Additional Information and Resources

material covered in this book. We encourage our readers to use this website to explore more about learning!

I also provide additional learning ideas and tips on Instagram: robertkkamei. These tips will add to your solid foundation about learning that you now possess from reading this book. If you or someone you know is interested in hearing more about learning, then take a look and share the site with others!

ROBERTKKAMEI

Index

active learning, 68, 145, 147
aspirational goals, 27–30, 34, 35, 159
attention, 59, 107, 110, 111

Bloom's Taxonomy, 73, 74
breaks, 107, 112–114

chunking, 52, 53, 61
connections, 49, 51–57, 61, 63, 66, 75
cramming, 77–79, 82

demotivation, 96–99
depth of processing, 67, 68, 76, 144
    shallow vs deep, 73–75
desirable difficulties, 71, 72
distractions, 110, 111, 113

Ebbinghaus, 45, 59, 63
    flattening the forgetting curve, 47, 63–75
    forgetting curve, 45–47, 63, 64, 75, 77, 80, 82, 87
    resetting the forgetting curve, 47, 77–87
Edu-tainment, 60
effort, 109, 118
encoding, 46, 47, 49–61
    specificity principle, 55, 56, 59, 61, 66
environment, 28, 55, 59
exercise, 114, 115, 119

feedback, 32
first principles, 150
Five Whys, 97–99, 125
flipped classroom, 142

goal setting, 21–34, 86, 91, 94, 96, 98, 99, 101, 104
Goldilocks and the Three Bears, 30, 31
growth vs. fixed mindset, 156

health, 107, 108, 110, 113–115, 117, 119

Index

Holistic Learning Framework, 11, 14–16, 18, 23, 38, 91, 108, 129

if-then statements, 101, 148
interleaving, 69–72, 76

learning, 21, 24, 25, 31, 34, 52, 55, 57–61, 63, 64, 66–87, 137–139, 141–149, 151
    learning sciences, 139, 142, 143, 146, 151
    personal learning plan, 17, 35, 134–136
lifelong learning, 138

McGurk effect, 50
memory, 38–47, 49–56, 59, 61
    long-term, 40, 41
    short-term, 38, 40, 41
metacognition, 12
Metacognitive Cycle, 15, 16, 37, 49, 63, 77, 86, 87
    evaluate, 16, 124, 129–131, 133
    implement, 16, 124, 128
    plan, 15, 86, 87
mnemonics, 53–55, 61, 66
motivation, 91–94, 96, 98, 99, 102, 104
    Internal vs External, 92–94
multitasking, 112, 113
music, 111, 112

Pareto Principle, 80
passive learning, 68

performance, 109, 115
problem-based learning, 142
procrastination, 99, 100, 101, 148
Proust effect, 55
purposeful practice, 86

recall vs recognition, 40–44
retrieval practice, 84–87
rote memory, 39, 51, 52
routine, 101–104

self-discipline, 78, 80, 90, 91, 97–99, 101, 104
self-regulation, 87, 89–91, 102
sleep, 107, 115–120
SMART goals, 25, 27, 28, 30, 31, 33, 34
social determinants of learning, 18
spaced learning, 77, 78, 82–84, 87
stereotype threat, 157
strategy, 80, 82, 84, 158, 159
study groups, 125–128

team-based learning, 142
teamwork skills, 143

wellbeing, 91, 107, 108, 120

virtual classroom, 147–149
Vygotsky, 31

Zone of Proximal Development, 31

www.ingramcontent.com/pod-product-compliance
Lightning Source LLC
Chambersburg PA
CBHW061940220426
43662CB00012B/1976